The Emotional Meaning
of Money

The Emotional Meaning of Money

Lewis Yablonsky, Ph.D.

Gardner Press, Inc
New York   London

Gardner Press, Inc.
19 Union Square West
New York, NY 10003

Distributed in Canada by:
Book Center, Inc.
1140 Beaulac Street
Montreal, Quebec H4R 1R8

Library of Congress Cataloging-in-Publication Data

Yablonsky, Lewis.
  The emotional meaning of money / by Lewis Yablonsky.
  212 p.   cm.
  Includes bibliographical references (p.   ).
  ISBN 0-89876-169-7
  1. Money—Social aspects—United States.   2. Money—United States—
-Psychological aspects.   I. Title.
HG501.Y33   1991
332.4'973—dc20   90-33366
                                                       CIP

Printed and bound in Canada

Book Design by Sidney Solomon

9   8   7   6   5   4   3   2   1

Contents

Preface and Acknowledgments

*H*OW ARE some billionaires and some homeless poor people alike in their attitudes about money? Many people in these two categories have a pathological relationship to money. Some billionaires can never get enough from their wheeling and dealing; and some poor homeless people have an emotional block to acquiring enough money to satisfy the basic necessities of their lives.

Money is, of course, power. Some people can't get enough and some do not want any. The paradox about money, however, is that it is not simply the amount you have that determines your power. Your power with money is regulated by whether you are in charge of your wealth or it controls you. Being in appropriate control of a small amount of money can make you a happier, more fulfilled person than being under the domination of vast amounts of money. Understanding this principle, and learning from the experiences of other people about how they manage money in their lives, will help you more positively adjust your emotional relationship to money so that you can lead a happier more prosperous life.

In fact, I would contend that if everyone developed healthier attitudes about money, and how they earned it, many of our societal ills would disappear. Such major social problems as emotional stress, marital discord, job problems, parent-child conflict, wars carried out on behalf of economic interests, and destructive economic competition would be significantly resolved in the larger society. The old saw "the love of money is the root of all evil" is substantiated by my book.

This book is based on data obtained from my two professional roles: psychotherapist and research sociologist. As a psychotherapist for forty years, I have plumbed the variety of emotional issues people have with money as it relates to their family, friends, and personal problems. In my role as sociologist, I have carried out research into people's relationships to money through over 50 in-depth interviews and a representative survey of 410 people from around the United States on their attitudes toward and emotional connections to money. The information obtained in my social research into money is woven into the overall fabric of the book. Readers specifically interested in my research approach and statistical data on people's attitudes toward money are invited to read the appendix, "Research Notes on Attitudes About Money."

Part I of the book, "The Emotional Power of Money," discusses people's individual money styles and attitudes about money from the point of view of gender, marriage, and parenting. Part II of the book, "Money Talks," presents interviews gathered from significant categories of people in our society including the superwealthy, poor people, deviants, creative people, artists, and people in the helping professions.

I am grateful to the many therapeutic clients, psychotherapists, social scientists, students, and other respondents who helped provide the data which is the spine of the book. In particular, I want to acknowledge the enormous contribution of my writer-colleague Melissa Sands, who in addition to closely editing the manuscript, added a substantial amount of data and insights, which improved the overall book.

Lewis Yablonsky, Ph.D.
DEPARTMENT OF SOCIOLOGY
CALIFORNIA STATE UNIVERSITY, NORTHRIDGE, CALIFORNIA

Part I

The Emotional Power of Money

1

Emotions and Money

> The world is too much with us.
> Getting and spending we lay waste our powers.
> — William Wordsworth

*M*ONEY SAYS a great deal about our personalities, our hopes and fears, our values, and our hang-ups. Money is hardly just an economic concept. From a person's first infantile reaction to a shiny coin to the final decision surrounding a loved one's burial—should it be lavish or sparse—money is an emotional force. Even after death, if you have accumulated wealth, heirs may launch emotional battles over the money you couldn't take with you. Some people reach their hand out of the grave through their will to spank or caress their heirs.

Money is a social and a psychological concept. The coin of any realm has no intrinsic worth. Its only worth is what people project onto it; and often it pays for the basic lifestyle a person desires. Money is clearly an emotional entity.

A better understanding of money's emotional impact on your life is invaluable. Money is inextricably a part of your identity and your emotional life. Once you decipher its code you can help protect yourself from unnecessary psychic pain, avoid self-defeating money styles, monitor the way money affects your relationships to loved ones and enemies, and even achieve greater wealth from an appreciation of what you have.

The scope of money's emotional impact is vast. It influences—especially in a financially competitive society like ours—practically every human reaction. Consider these points:

↪ Most business is directed at profiting from every relationship and human interaction in the marketplace.

↪ Sexual attractiveness and gratification is enhanced by wealth and diminished in its absence. In a 1986 survey conducted by *Money* magazine of 2555 households, more cash equaled better sex according to one out of three adult Americans. In response to the question, "If you had more money, do you think your sex life would be better? 15 percent said yes, and another 18 percent said it might be. Of those who thought the rich have more fun in bed, 37 percent were men and 30 percent were women.

↪ Money often is pivotal to one's self-concept, self-esteem, and sense of intelligence. As Tevya sings in the classic musical play *Fiddler on the Roof,* "If I were a rich man . . . when you're rich people think you really know."

↪ Financial battles are at the heart of many family conflicts. Thirty-seven percent of the couples surveyed in the *Money* magazine poll admitted arguing over money in the last twelve months, making money *the* subject of most controversy.

↪ Friendship and selection of a romantic mate are often entwined with money. For example, a Rockefeller is never sure who is really a friend. Many wealthy people believe they are loved only for their money.

↪ Money often determines the length of time spent on or with a person, as in "Joe is a waste of time" and "Time is money."

↪ Money is a feature in peoples daydreams. I asked people, "Hypothetically, what would you do if you suddenly inherited a million dollars?" The question elicited a wide range of answers from the expected to the bizarre: "I would leave my wife immediately." "I would quit my job—and wreck the office." "I would quit seeing a psychiatrist." "I would buy out the company I work for and fire everyone there." "I would have the power to *get* my enemies." "I would open the perfect school and send my children to it." "I would design and build a car that wouldn't produce smog, and display it on a national tour."

From these fiscal windfall wishes it's clear money is imbued with enormous power. In fact, except for a few idealists, money is power. Even Webster defines success in monetary language: "The attainment of wealth; the termination of a venture."

In most societies, not just ours, money is a significant yardstick of measure of a person's success. Money is perceived by most people as the primary indicator of a person's status. Earned money accords power and success; however, inherited money too bathes a person in the attributes of success and power.

Given the way money is emotionally tied to personal success and power, it is hardly surprising to see how money equates to a person's sense of self-worth. When I asked people to tell me how money affects their emotional life, I found they invariably connected it to self-concept. This point was illustrated poignantly by a young aspiring actress. Her worth as a person was inextricably linked to dollars. As she explained, "If you're an actress, a successful actress, people imbue you with brilliance, with beauty, with class, with talent; and therefore you actually become what they see in you. It's like a mirror.

"My struggle all my life has been looking into mirrors, becoming what other people saw. In my parents' eyes I was not valuable, I was nothing. I felt worthless. If someone sees you as nothing, you become stupid, clumsy, ugly. In a book I read once about a transsexual who changed his name from Jim to Jan after undergoing a sex-change operation, I remember a quote: 'The more I was treated as a woman, the more of a woman I became. If I was assumed to be incompetent at backing out of a driveway in my car or opening a bottle, I became incompetent. If a case was thought to be too heavy for me to lift, inexplicably I found it so.'

"If I succeed as an actress and have lots of money, people will imbue me with knowledge, talent, and beauty. I could then overcome the damage my parents did, of devaluing me."

This young woman's self-image was as bound up with money as with other people's approval. In her mind, money was the emotional currency that could heal deep psychological scars. Money and fame were equated with the elevation of her status and identity. In some cases, money does indeed help improve a poor self-image. There is no insurance, though, that it will work such miracles for everyone. And status based on such a frail foundation is tenuous.

It's true (though not fair) that a person's value and status is often defined by the amount of money he or she earns, by that person in particular and by others as well. Rich people wear an aura of personal power; poor people are generally considered unsuccessful and power-less. A person's purity of character does not figure into these characterizations. Money, and money only, signals the stereotype.

Despite the claims that America is a "classless society," it is apparent that money establishes a strata of haves and have-nots. The more money you have, within certain limits, the more access you have to the status and lifestyle you desire. Money certainly buys the best medical care, food, clothes, and shelter.

Money means freedom from want and freedom to embrace a wide range of options. Poor peoples' lives are limited, closed in comparison to those of their wealthier counterparts. Affluent people have choice. They can change their appearance with clothes, plastic surgery, or with the aid of cosmetics, color, or fashion consultants. They can change spouses or find new romantic partners with less difficulty. Money enables a person to shift the responsibility of child care to nannies, baby-sitters, or maids. Life provides a wide array of possibilities with access depending on how much money one has.

Careers are often contingent upon money. Money buys venture capital in business. Money affords risk, which can lead to great and satisfying financial gain. This equation applies to all levels of workers. Consider the case of an actor I interviewed. His remarks point out how money affects professional independence and odds.

"I blame my failure to get good theatrical roles on the fact that I have no 'fuck-you money,' " he began indignantly. "'Fuck-you money' gives you independence. When you're broke most of the time like I am, you have to take any role that comes along, and you even think of a sleazy porno role, anything. If you have money, you can be selective and build your career your way."

Obviously, this situation is not restricted to actors, but applies to many other people engaged in the creative professions. Money and creativity are strange bedfellows indeed, an issue we'll focus on in a later chapter.

The final point about money buying professional success is summed up in one area—education. Financing your ambition and aspirations often comes down to your ability to finance your education, and with more money you can select the better schools. As the cost of education rises, and loan programs decrease, fewer people will be able to afford the cost of their career dreams.

Longevity, even survival, is determined to a great extent by money. In poorer countries, and in pockets of poverty within our own country, the infant mortality rate is higher and the life span shorter than in affluent countries and affluent segments of society. Correlations have consistently been found between infant mortality, longevity, and wealth.

Money enables all possible leisure activities, ranging from adventure and travel to artistic endeavors. Those of us affluent enough can scale mountain peaks or ski the Alps, lounge on the French Riviera, or balloon the Serengetty Plains in Africa. Those of us less affluent can't afford the personal adventure, we can only afford the price of a television for the relatively less satisfactory, vicarious thrill of watching. Social science research has not fully measured the negative impacts on the millions of people who no longer live their lives through direct experience but count on television.

One's philosophy of life and attitude about destiny is often described in relation to money. For example, people who are depressed by their poverty and powerlessness think, probably erroneously, that money will change everything. They assume increased wealth will propel them upward to a place where they will not only do better but feel better about themselves.

The "money-is-the-answer to life's problems" philosophy finds an interesting contact in those people who are afraid of money and its effects upon their lives. Since monetary changes are usually reflected in power shifts, some people consciously or unconsciously resist wealth. They may turn down lucrative deals or promotions in the workplace or handle their personal finances in self-defeating ways. The fear of money was illuminated by one of my respondents who said, "I'm happy with my current position in life. Even though I live on the financial margin, I'm happy with my wife and kids in my current home. Who knows what more wealth might bring? I might wind up divorced or estranged from my kids. I'm quite happy with my life now and don't want things to change. Money might throw me into another orbit. I'm careful not to accumulate too much."

Wealth as a harbinger of doom was a classic belief during the 1960s among a generation of hippies. Tens of thousands of young people joined a counterculture movement which eschewed money and materialism in exchange for various theories of peace and love. The back-to-nature posture of a rebellious generation was a reaction for many against their families, who had money but lacked happiness.

As one young dropout lamented during an interview I did for my book *The Hippie Trip*:

"My mom and dad are rich. They have everything this society can give them: a beautiful home, cars, European vacations, and yet I see them as miserable people. They are always fighting and they always want more. I don't want to grow up and be as miserable as they are! So I left home and live in Haight-Ashbury. I'm looking for a lifestyle that doesn't have dollars printed all over it."[1]

Moreover, antimoney postures and sentiments are not characteristic only of hippies, renegades, and revolutionaries. Children of wealth often attempt to avoid their inherited wealthy status, as we'll see in the chapter on the rich.

Money can be seen as the be-all or the end-all, and opinions on both sides of this coin can be highly emotional and irrational. Curious attitudes abound. To make the point, I'll tell you about a peculiar incident. My wife and I were at a restaurant with an old friend. One of his friends joined us for lunch. In the course of conversation children were mentioned and we brought up our son, who was of course at that time, the most beautiful child on the planet. My wife had a picture ready to prove our point and was poised to show the picture to our new acquaintance. As politely as he could, this man refused to look at our snapshot, explaining, "That's one of the things I don't do anymore. I recently inherited quite a bit of money. I no longer talk to certain people, and one thing I never do anymore is look at people's baby pictures."

Although his rude behavior didn't endear him to us personally, his point about how money can change people's behavioral patterns was a valuable lesson.

Another curiosity is how effectively money can be an aphrodisiac. I was at the home of a successful screenwriter, at a dinner party with a group of about ten people. We were discussing the ins and outs of the Hollywood scene. Our host mentioned in passing that he'd just sold a screenplay for a record figure, several hundred thousand dollars. Some of us in the group, including myself, responded with mixed emotions, congratulating him on his coup but also resentful of his chintzy bragging air. However, I noticed one young lady in the group reacted to his announcement with great emotion. She gasped, her face flushed, and she shook her head in mock disbelief. Given my research interest in money and its emotional linkage, I made a point of interviewing her later that evening. She confessed, "When he mentioned all that money, my reaction was a sexual surge, it pulsed right through me. I never really paid much attention to Bob [the screenwriter], but when he mentioned that colossal fee, he looked suddenly absolutely handsome to me and I became very sexually aroused."

In the course of my surveys I found this was no isolated case. Here is another story in which the feel of money was definitely sexy. This woman's explanation of events leading up to her marriage says it all: "I had been out with Hal several times. Actually I found him quite dull and boring. He wasn't particularly handsome either. I had a dinner date with him, and I was all set to make it our last. He has his own business and on our last date I had agreed to come by his office. It was downright palatial! This was the first time I saw Hal in his own environment. A very powerful person he was, seated behind an enormous desk. He said, 'Give me a few minutes to sign these payroll checks.' As he sat there signing those checks I looked on and had this unexpected erotic sensation. He looked better, sexier, than I had ever seen him. I wanted him right then and there. I could hardly keep my hands off him until we went to bed together that night. A month later I married Hal."

Whether or not Hal married a bonafide gold digger is disputable. What is indisputable is that for many people money is a turn-on. Poverty likewise can be a turn-off. Just ask single men, who resent en masse the most popular question put to them when they meet a woman in a social situation: "What do you do for a living?", a question intended by some women to separate the money-making men from the poor boys.

The importance of money to certain people borders on neurosis, if not more severe psychopathology. Money plays a significant role in emotional problems. An examination of the news on almost any day reveals extreme or bizarre scenarios relating to the acquisition of money. According to one story in the *Los Angeles Times:*

> Ronald C. O'Bryan was convicted of murder Tuesday in the Halloween candy poisoning of his eight-year-old son. The prosecution contended that O'Bryan gave his son, Timothy, cyanide-laced candy last Halloween eve to collect more than $30,000 in life insurance money. The boy died in painful convulsions at a Houston hospital a few hours after eating the candy.[2]

If greed and desperation fueled Ronald O'Bryan's dastardly deed, greed also motivated the infamous Hetty Green. Although she was a millionairess several times over, she tried to have her son's infected leg treated at a charity hospital. Rebuffed, she chose to allow the condition to worsen, to the point where her only son lost his leg. This occurred despite the fact that she was worth millions, and could easily have afforded the best available medical care.

Many millionaires have exhibited gross stinginess and eccentricities in relation to how they manage their fortunes. Periodically, true *National Enquirer* type stories come to light. One example was the Collier Brothers. When they died after years of living in filth and poverty, they left an untouched fortune behind.

In this context, who can adequately explain the pathological driving force behind people like Donald Trump, who already has a fortune that can't be spent in ten lifetimes, to acquire more and more and more? Or the wealthy Marcos family, who looted the Philippine treasury for untold millions.

Some psychotherapists suggest financial neuroses are tied into emotional deprivation in early childhood. Freud propounded an elaborate theory wherein the handling of money was related to retention and expulsion of feces. He wrote extensively on money and emotional issues, defining what he called an anal-retentive personality type. According to his theory, in simplistic terms, parsimonious people were somehow locked into an anal stage of life, and this made them pathologically acquisitive.

Dr. James Knight, in his book *For the Love of Money,* traced the connection between money and excrement in myth and language. Fairy tales like "The Goose That Laid the Golden Egg" are cited. Linguistic expressions like "stinking rich" and "filthy miser" support his theories. Gamblers' slang, he feels, is especially noteworthy: the stakes being "the pot," dice being "craps," lucky players being described as "cleaning up," or "falling into a barrel of crap."[3]

If one chooses to make the wild psychoanalytical leap, to which I don't necessarily subscribe, relating money to excrement, it becomes relevant to toilet training conflicts. Children whose training is traumatic or overly severe may develop revengeful and defiant traits relating to retaining or withholding. These conflicts may surface in behaviors which feature hoarding or greed.

In my own therapeutic work with money-sick people over the years, I have definitely seen a complex relationship between their money ideology and neurosis. However, in my observations, the cases were simpler than the tortured and circumlocutory psychoanalyses of Freud and his disciples.

I recall the case of a young woman who turned in her therapy with a professional counselor for a session with a salesperson. She told me in one session, "I usually felt better after talking with my psychiatrist. He told me I had a 'deprivation syndrome.' This meant because of my deprived childhood I would get depressed when I couldn't buy what I wanted.

"One week I called in sick and played hookey on my therapist. I let him know sufficiently in advance so there was no charge. Then I took the hundred dollars he would get and bought myself a Gucci wallet at a fancy Beverly Hills boutique. The high I felt from buying that wallet made me feel much happier than my usual boring session with the psychiatrist. I quit seeing him.

"Now I buy myself one or two special things every other week. I know I'm not solving my basic problem, but I feel better than when I was seeing the therapist."

Therapists may take issue with this young woman's self-help prescription, but perhaps she knew her needs best. She was right on the mark in recognizing how spending made her "feel" better, even though it was only a maintenance program that would never resolve her core emotional problem.

Just as we now recognize the connection between shopaholics and ego gratification, we recognize gambling as being emotionally tied to a person's ego. While more on gambling will be included in the chapter on deviance and dollars, let me include a few remarks here from a fifty-five-year-old bookie who soldered hustling dollars with mother love early in his gambling career.

"What money means to me? Are you kidding? It's been my whole life. The things I've had to do for a good score. Like when I was a kid— my father cut out when I was five. Who knows where the creep went. Well, anyway, money was the main thing between me and my mother. When I was around thirteen and old enough to hustle a few bucks, and I brought it to her, her face would light up with joy. She would say, 'I hope you didn't do anything wrong,' but I knew when I gave her a little dough—even a few bucks—she really loved me. Since that time, having money has always meant good feelings and love."

This young boy grew into a veteran hustler for whom gambling became an obsession. The key to understanding his obsessive behavior lies in recognizing his emotional shorthand for money. Money meant love and approval; gambling meant access to those; therefore, all three components were blurred into a singular life quest.

While this is not to say *all* gamblers are neurotic and obsessive, it is a safe enough inference to say most gambling behavior has emotional egocentric motives and a compulsive quality. How else can we explain the unfortunate downfall of baseball's Pete Rose. He must have known on some level that his compulsive gambling would finally negatively affect his status in his beloved game.

The challenge of money is not merely how to obtain it. The real challenge is how to recognize and separate rational and irrational reactions surrounding finances. An important positive side effect of money to many people is that it does provide a certain amount of real power and security for a predictable future.

People's attitudes toward credit, so basic to our economy, can also be emotionally laden, in both positive and negative ways. Home ownership depends upon it for most people, who necessarily interact with banks and credit organizations to acquire this most crucial lifetime investment. Credit is at the heart of modern commerce. In contemporary society, hardly a venture is undertaken or a transaction made, from furnishing a home to building a nuclear reactor, without the reality of credit.

In my research, I found that people have a wide range of emotional reactions to credit. Some are realistic. They value credit, treat it with respect, and are grateful for all the possibilities a good credit rating grants. Others exhibit a subtle terror toward credit establishments which control their plastic purse strings.

People whose credit cards have been abused and consequently withdrawn, talk about feelings of deep humiliation. One fairly affluent man related this experience: "I hit this dry period financially and my cash flow dried up. I couldn't pay my bills. I wrote letters asking for delays and, surprisingly, in some cases organizations deferred payments. But the credit card companies were cold-blooded robots. My Carte Blanche and American Express cards were canceled by letter. The most humiliating experience of my life occurred one morning when I heard the doorbell ring at 7:00 A.M.! Standing at the door of my $250,000 home was a Bankamericard messenger who coldly announced, 'I've come to get your card.' I wanted to tell him to go fuck himself, but I got scared. I thought I'd better comply or the police would arrive next. With inner fear and trembling I ran to my wallet and handed over my credit card. For days I felt frightened, depressed, and humiliated. I've never been bankrupt, but I felt that's what happened to me. I don't think I got my self-respect back until I got my Bankamericard back a year later. I felt I had to do it to regain my sense of identity."

It is apparent to me from stories like these that there are at least two basic attitudes toward money: a rational one and an irrational, emotional one. A rational assessment of money recognizes that it can maximize your life, affording security, material benefits, opportunities that range from educational to aesthetic and recreational, and a comfortable retirement in the later years. It is natural and understandable to pursue money for all of these reasons. Unrealistic attitudes prevail when money borders on being an obsession and behaviors relating to it become neurotic or pathological.

The way to begin to assess your attitudes toward money is to identify the emotional meanings you attach to it. There is a distinct feel to money and it's not the metallic feel of coin or the crisp feel of paper. Money feels different to different people. As you've seen, money "feels" good or bad, powerful or restricting, hopeful or depressing, exhilarating, sexy, or frightening. Knowing that you attach personal emotions to money will give you a better understanding of the role money plays in your life and personal happiness.

Money can be gratifying or defeating, depending on your "money-style." My research has uncovered some basic money-styles that people have adopted in their lives. These patterns will be discussed next, and I'm sure you'll recognize your personal approach to money in one of the following chapters.

2

Money Styles

Money is a living thing. It grows with time.
Money is my child, my future life. When
I am one with money, I am immortal.
— Commentary from an actor in the
role of a psychopathic religious
leader in the Japanese film,
A Taxing Woman's Return
(1989)

*M*ONEY IS an inescapable part of everyone's life.
Everyone learns some means to acquire money and develops patterns
for spending it. Your relationship with money, your hows and whys of
getting and spending, add up to your personal money style.

Money style flows from the basic personality of a person. Since
money is so pivotal an issue, how you handle your money bears a
striking resemblance to how you handle other issues, like love and
affection. For example, people who are tight, acquisitive, and retentive
about money usually behave the same way in their human relationships. Someone who has difficulty parting with his or her money is
likely to display an inability to give affection as well.

Your money style reveals a lot about your personal success and
power. The relationship among money, success, and power in your life
predicts how you rate the meaning of your life. Your satisfaction or

dissatisfaction with life hangs on how you cast your money style. Your money style also dictates just how important a role money plays in the emotions of your life. In essence, knowing your money style is very important in learning about yourself and your own road to happiness.

In my research, I identified five basic money styles, or ways people adapt to making and spending money. These were developed from analyzing fifty in-depth interviews and assessing the 410 people interviewed through a questionnaire. Although I've attached labels here, I was careful not to use these labels initially in my questions, so as not to influence the responses of the participants. Once I arrived at the five money styles I polled all my survey participants to classify themselves. Here are the results:

1. The Contented

"I am generally content with whatever my money, power, and success position happens to be." That statement was checked off by 105 people, or 25 percent of my population.

Fred is a retired claims supervisor for an international company manufacturing paper products. He worked at his job for forty years, unplagued by burning ambition to rise to the top of the corporate ladder and garner a six-figure salary. He was happy with his family and his ability to buy a house and live "better than his parents" did. His wife didn't have to go to work, they both felt they had it all, or enough of it to make him content with his breadwinning status.

Fred is a good example of the Contented posture, perfectly pleased with his money, power, and success status.

2. Logical Achievers

"I have logical and achievable financial-power-success goals and can acquire or have the financial success I seek." That statement was checked off by 94 people, or 24 percent.

The main characteristic of this group is that their goals are realistic and achievable, safe and solid aspirations as opposed to idealistic or pie-in-the-sky strivings.

Glenda is such a person. Although she came from a lower class position in society, Glenda always wanted to be a teacher. She loved books and playing school as a child, and wanting to become a teacher was a natural outgrowth of that. Although her parents had not attended college, they encouraged Glenda, who, with hard work and scholarship assistance, did indeed become the teacher she had always wanted to be.

Glenda is very pleased with her profession, her salary, and herself. Like the other Logical Achievers, she had a reasonable goal in relation to her status; she sought a specific new status and reached it.

3. Emotionally Unaffected Strivers

"I strive to attain all of the money, power, and success I can attain, yet I do not let my money struggle, nor my success or lack of success, negatively affect my emotional condition." Eighty-six of the participants felt they fit that category, or 21 percent.

Bill started out selling shoes when he was a teenager. At the time he didn't know that the retail business would figure into his life scheme, but it did. He did know he wanted to be a millionaire, but exactly how he was going to reach that pinnacle was never clearly pictured in his mind.

Bill eventually went to work in the shoe department of a large Chicago department store, first managing the other sales personnel in the department, then moving into the buying end. On one of his European buying assignments he came across a new Italian designer, who had great designs but a not-so-great financial situation. Bill decided to take several thousand dollars he had saved and invest in this young Italian's fashion sense.

Five years later, Bill was the president of a fashion import business specializing in shoes and handbags, belts and scarves, doing a million dollars of sales annually. He was not a millionaire yet, but was definitely on his way.

The most salient thing about Bill's money style was that he had learned early on to separate his professional life from his personal life. During the risky years, he often told his wife that if worse came to worst he could always go back into the retail department store business. "Nothing ventured, nothing gained" was a personal motto that kept his fear of failing manageable and his home life tranquil.

Bill is a good example of the Emotionally Unaffected Striver, because although he aspired to great wealth, he didn't let his struggle negatively affect his personal or emotional life.

4. The Emotionally Affected Strivers

"I aggressively strive for an ideal and possibly achievable *high* level of financial power and success, and suffer emotional pain because I have not achieved my desired goal of financial power and success." Fifty-six people or 14 percent checked off that category as descriptive of their money style.

Laura, a female journalist, fit this type. She was in college majoring in English when she saw the film *All the President's Men.* From that moment on she knew what she wanted out of life. She wanted to break a colossally big scandal, write a best-seller, and acquire fame and fortune in one fell swoop. And she wanted it to happen yesterday.

Being in such a hurry to make it to the fast track distorted Laura's growth. Instead of feeling pride when she landed her first reporter's spot, she felt frustrated because it was on a local southwestern paper, not the *New York Times.* She moved around the country from one newspaper to another within a decade, and rather than feeling a growing sense of accomplishment, she felt a gnawing sense of failure at still being in the boondocks. Laura passed on relationships with several good men because she felt her ambition was much more important.

By the time Laura hit thirty-five she was practically suicidal. She had created a few good stories, but never good enough to catapult her to the star-journalist status she sought. She felt disgusted with her life, even though for all intents and purposes she had a good job, a comfortable salary, and a promising future. From the point of view of her exaggerated expectations, she'd failed. She had worked for nearly fifteen years, twenty-four hours a day, never spent any energy making friends or soldering romantic relationships—and for what? Her high hopes of fame and glory were still out of reach.

The main feature that makes Laura a typical Emotionally Affected Striver is her sense of suffering. There is nothing self-sabotaging about reaching for the stars in our Horatio Alger society, but there is something very self-defeating about not being able to give one's self credit for smaller successes in life.

5. The Insatiables

"The next level of money, power, and success I seek always seems to be the next level up the ladder. There always seems to be a gap between what I want and what I have. I am usually in a state of emotional pain, and have a sense of deprivation no matter what I seem to get." Sixty-seven respondents felt that statement described their money style, about 16 percent of the total population in my study.

To look at Paul was to look at the American success story. He wore the most expensive suits he could buy, or rather that his wife could find when she wasn't having others made special. He drove a Mercedes, half of a pair—one for him and the other for his wife. There wasn't a posh vacation spot, or "in" restaurant he wasn't familiar with. He was considered one of the finest, brightest minds in entertainment law. He owned a palatial home in Beverly Hills and a penthouse overlooking Central Park in New York. The million dollar questions were "Why wasn't Paul satisfied?" and "Why didn't his two teen-age kids want to grow up to be like him?"

Paul was fond of saying he'd never be happy. He knew himself well. He hadn't been happy as a child, living in a poor neighborhood with alcoholic parents. He hadn't been happy in school even though he'd always been near the top of every class. He hadn't been happy working in other prestigious law firms first as a clerk, then as a partner. He hadn't been happier going out on his own, even though clients flocked to him. No matter how much money, status, or prestige he acquired, he knew it could never wipe out some insatiable gnawing deep within.

After his kids told him during a heated battle that he was a miserable man and they never wanted to be like him, he finally began listening to his wife, who had recommended therapy. She had been telling him for years that someone who worked so hard deserved a little happiness, and he blocked it off. Perhaps a counselor could help him find some satisfaction in life before it was too late.

Insatiables like Paul carry a never-ending burden of pain and deprivation which is totally illogical in view of the money/success/ power they have achieved. It's as if they have an infinite void somewhere in their psyche, and though they are driven to fill it with accomplishment, prestige, and dollars, they can never do enough and they remain forever unfulfilled.

DISTRIBUTION OF MONEY STYLES ON THE ECONOMIC LADDERS

For the rest of our discussion, I'll refer to the first three styles—Contented, Logical Achievers, and Unaffected Emotional Achievers—generally as "Contenteds" and to the last two styles—Affected Emotional Strivers and Insatiables—as "Insatiables." I want to keep my labels simple so you don't miss a surprising, important point. Originally, I assumed that a person's financial status would determine unequivocally his or her money style. I thought Insatiable types would tend to be wealthier because they were so driven, and that their insatiable drive would fuel them well past their Contented counterparts. Contrary to that hypothesis, I found that the *amount* of money people had was *not* a measure of insatiability or contentment.

I found equal numbers of Contenteds and Insatiables existing on all rungs of the economic ladder! Neither net worth, age, nor occupation absolutely determined fiscal contentment or the lack of it. In other words, the poor have the same odds on fiscal satisfaction as the rich. Both wealth and poverty can account for misery or fulfillment depending on one's money adaptation.

I checked my finding several ways. I ranked people according to income in gradations of $20,000 to $30,000 per year, and up to $100,000 and over. I found approximately the same breakdown, 70 percent Contenteds and 30 percent Insatiables, in each category. The data was further analyzed by age, educational level, and gender, and the same proportions of money styles in each category were found.

The finding that the majority of people were content with their money/power/success situation, some 70 percent, corresponds with another finding related to occupational motives: 80 percent of the respondents claimed money was a secondary, not primary, motive for the occupation in which they worked. Since work can be the medium of expression for the money style, this finding further backs up a surprising fiscal picture.

How can it be that poor people can be just as "satisfied" as rich people, and conversely that rich people can be just as "miserable about their lot" as poor people? Adopting a sociological outlook helps to explain this phenomenon.

People seek out and adapt to their own peer group. The group to which they belong also becomes a reference for measuring their own success. For example, people in the $20,000 to $30,000 income bracket have their own social milieu. Within this category, a $29,000-a-year earner is "upper class," and a $20,000-a-year earner is "lower class." Obviously, the person in this bracket is not measuring his or her success/power/money position by the same standards used by a $100,000-a-year earner. Those upper income folks have a different level of aspiration.

A person's level of aspiration is defined by the limits within his group. In a sense, people attempt to keep up with the Joneses or the Rockefellers, depending on their identification. For example, if the $29,000-a-year earner was measuring success in comparison to the standards of a $100,000 earner, a great sense of emotional deprivation would be the end result, not a sense of contentment. Our society would be a lot more disturbed as a whole if everyone aspired to achieve the status of a Rockefeller or a Donald Trump. In this context, a larger segment of the population would become severely insatiable, exhibiting a continuing sense of pain.

As it stands now, people in each stratum have their own level of aspiration and it is their money style, not their group membership, that determines insatiable feelings or contented ones. For instance, the person who lives in an $80,000 home will be happy with that if he is in the 70 percent Contenteds group. However, if he's an Insatiable, his level of aspiration will keep rising. When he affords the $150,000 home, he'll aspire to the $200,000 home. When he gets that one, the $300,000 will be "needed." An escalating level of aspiration is what frustrates Insatiables of all strata; a relative level of aspiration, and a stationary one, is what keeps Contenteds in all financial brackets happy.

To further test my hypothesis I met with a group of twenty-five black, relatively poor, people in the Watts neighborhood of Los Angeles, a socioeconomically disadvantaged area. In the course of our discussions, I tried to stir them up on the theme of "status frustration," attitudes many people project onto this segment of the population. We assume that status frustration propels many poor people to deviant lives of crime and drugs. At one point I commented, "We've been talking about money all night and you all seem fairly content to accept the fact of your money situation. Aren't you angry about all the rich people in this town in Bel Air and Beverly Hills who have all the money?"

Most of the Watts twenty-five responded with limited anger. They fit into the overall model of my findings. They were content because they gave little thought to their upper-socioeconomic-level neighbors. They were concerned with their own peers. Mainly they talked about their financial status in connection with "brothers and sisters" in their own neighborhood. Statistically, 70 percent were Contenteds, either relating to the Contented, Logical Achievers, or Emotionally Unaffected Striver categories.

Several young men in the group did take an expected hostile approach, saying, "I am pissed off about being black and poor. And I have ripped off some rich mothers. Whenever I get a chance I will beat them by any means necessary to get their money. That's my own way of getting even. I don't understand how any of my brothers or sisters can be content about their poverty!"

It is unfair to have such fiscal disparity in America. It's fortunate that people in the poor position adapt or we'd be in a state of eternal revolution until money inequities were resolved.

THE DRIVING FORCES BEHIND INSATIABILITY

The logic of the Watts complacency with regard to money is less surprising when contrasted with some cases of the "miserable rich." Take the greed king and queen of the 80s, Leona and Harry Helmsley, billionaire hotel entrepreneurs who were convicted of major tax fraud and extortion. Beneath the scandal is the behavior of two classic rich Insatiable millionaires. Various interviews with their employees in their hotels, secretaries, and in-laws, characterize both Leona and Harry as ruthless, obsessed with money, and neurotic, despite separate and joint fortunes. Leona even managed to co-opt her late son's estate, leaving only a paltry $432 for each of four grandchildren, and an eviction notice for his widow! Trying to welsh the government in similar priggish fashion, by evading four million in income taxes and deducting "business expenses" like a $130,000 indoor-outdoor pool, and birthday gifts like a $45,000 hotel-shaped silver clock and assorted other jewels, clothes, etcetera, landed them in deep trouble.[1]

How could two such superwealthy "skinflints" conduct themselves like this? The key to their stinginess lies in a money style that told them "it's never enough." The old "you can never be too rich" philosophy made them dissatisfied with a fortune they could *never* spend in several lifetimes, and brought misery to many of those around them too!

Some Insatiables have a neurotic drive. Neurotically driven Insatiables often prove to have had excessively deprived, poverty-stricken childhoods. Early on, material things were equated with love. They are set on a course to acquire money and objects to fill an "emotional hole," but no amount of cars, clothes, or cash will ever satiate their deep psychic needs.

Another explanation for this neurotic drive is warped values. Some people are taught during childhood: You are what you have, and only money is power. Psychiatrists' offices and psychiatric literature are teeming with such stories. In Budd Schulburg's classic book *What Makes Sammy Run?*, Sammy is the archetypal poor American, insatiably driven because he has been taught that financial success is the goal. In his quest he runs over anyone who gets in his way. After achieving enormous success, Sammy confronts himself and finds his life empty, mirroring an all-too-frequent real-life melodrama. Yet the book's lesson still eludes him: Humanism is more important than materialism. This message is, perhaps, *not* one many of us teach our children well.

Some Insatiables are "stuck" in a childhood stage. Most children and teenagers are at first normally insatiable. They are generally hedonistic, desirous of many material things. At this developmental stage they rarely see beyond their own individual needs. And they have a limited understanding of how money is acquired and dispensed. Often they will cry, cajole, or con their parents to get what they want. How parents respond will eventually determine the child's pattern and relationship with money.

In Chapter 5, I will focus on parenting and learning about money. Suffice it to say here, children who receive consistent and appropriate monetary instructions will mature out of this insatiable stage into a more mature money posture. Children who receive inappropriate monetary instructions will become adults for whom money is a frustrating, loaded issue. As adults, if they are not granted their every whim, they can feel angry and as if they have been cheated.

For both the neurotic and the childish Insatiable types, money and the things money can buy offer only temporary relief from emotional pain. Their hunger is constant. Despite their feeding it, it rises up and demands more constantly.

Compulsive shoppers provide a good example of this kind of ravenous appetite. They shop at the most exclusive stores, within their own definition. It could be Sears or Rodeo Drive, depending on their social class. The immediate "fix," akin to a drug addict's, is buying something exclusive and unique for a lower than usual price. This makes them feel special, assuaging a characteristic low self-esteem. The item delivers prestige, status, worth. However, the good feeling doesn't last; the item quickly becomes old hat. Another purchase is "needed" to quell the longing. Purchases come and go; the appetite remains.

No doubt, fashion houses from Sears-Roebuck to Christian Dior (consciously or unconsciously) pander to the insatiable component in all of us as they design new fashions each season, making last year's unfashionably out.

An Insatiable money style can be harmful to the individual but is usually relatively harmless to society. The one exception is the type I would call the Insatiable Money-Psychopath. Although I haven't conclusively proven this connection in my research, I will venture to suggest that an Insatiable Money-Psychopath criminality go hand in hand. In my survey, criminals, drug addicts, and gamblers had higher insatiable percentages than most people.

In order to discuss the Insatiable Money-Psychopath, it is first necessary to define the concept of the psychopath. Dr. Harvey Cleckley, a psychiatrist and expert in the field, defines the psychopath as follows:

> This term refers to chronically antisocial individuals who are always in trouble, profiting neither from experience nor punishment, and maintaining no real loyalties to any person, group, or code. They are frequently callous, showing marked emotional immaturity, with lack of responsibility, lack of judgment, and an ability to rationalize their behavior so that it appears warranted, reasonable, and justified.[1]

A Money-Psychopath differs from a neurotically money-oriented person because he or she has (a) a limited social conscience, (b) egocentric behavior including manipulating others for his or her aim, (c) inability to forgo immediate pleasure for future goals, and (d) a habit of pathological lying. This combination of traits adds up to a character and moral disorder. Money-Psychopaths go after money using any means necessary. They are often criminals or deviant individuals, but can be white-collar professionals, politicians, and business people, too.

What makes a person an Insatiable Money-Psychopath is a selfish egocentric drive for money, and his or her willingness to do anything, even brutalize others, to acquire it. Often they rationalize their behavior in self-serving ways. A good contemporary example is found in the recent rash of corporate raiders who justify heavily lining their own pockets with the rationalization that they are "helping" the companies they plunder.

Not all Insatiables are Money-Psychopaths, but all Money-Psychopaths are Insatiable. Their money needs are continuous, callous, and impervious to controls, both the inner controls of conscience and the outer control of laws. They are doubly dangerous, to themselves psychologically and to society as a whole.

As you can see, your money style, and the money style of others, is a significant issue. Classifying your money posture and understanding your relationship with money is important.

What happens if you have a self-defeating money style? Can you change it? Yes, money styles can change throughout life, either through the course of events, or with some self-awareness and self-determination.

One survey respondent told of how his son's death catapulted him from an Insatiable money/power/success track into a more reasonable posture toward money. "My son was killed in Viet Nam. That terrible event changed my way of life. When I received that news from the Army, my life became meaningless for a long time. It took a year before I could think about anything else. I'm a businessman who always concentrated on making money. After my son's death it wasn't the same. My work went on, but I lost my drive to make a fortune."

In this case, the horrendous impact of his son's death derailed the man's Insatiable money style. Other, more humanistic things in his life gained precedence.

It doesn't take a catastrophe of epic proportion to adjust a self-sabotaging money style. Just the realization that the way you see money is catastrophic to your peace of mind could be enough to get you to change.

The bottom line is: It's not how much you have, but how you feel about it. Right now, your money style is either an asset or a liability. Remember, though, financial satisfaction is affordable to anyone, regardless of tax bracket. Your net worth, after all, is meaningless if it doesn't make you happy.

CHAPTER

3

Women, Men, and Money

A FEW DECADES ago, in most cases, the facts of American life cast the man in an independent money position as the breadwinner, and the woman in a dependent money position as the housewife and mother. There was a clear division of labor: His work domain was outside the home and *paid,* hers was inside and *unpaid.*

Both men and women were conditioned from early childhood to grow into those roles. Most parents perceived their newborn boy as having potential to support himself so long as he was properly socialized with the work ethic. In contrast, most newborn girls were perceived in different terms, not as having earning potential but the potential to attract an earner. Girls were reared to groom and adorn themselves so they could get married and raise a family—women's work, women's destiny.

There was very little in the culture that disputed this "natural monetary order" of male dominance and female dependence. History supported it with dowries. Cultural anthropology supported it with bride sales and female infanticide, an extreme measure practiced to purge primitive groups of too many dependent mouths. But in recent years, the wave of feminism has challenged this old economic status quo for men and women.

Women like Freda would never be the same. Her interview was conducted at the beginning of my research and illustrates the old money language spoken between the sexes.

"Some girlfriends of mine who are into women's lib think I should pay more attention to our money situation. But Mark and I have a good marriage. I'd rather concern myself with taking care of the house and the kids, and leave the money matters to Mark. It works quite well for us. In our family Mark is the head of the household, and although we often discuss financial matters, he makes all the final decisions. After all, he knows a lot more about it than I do.

"My parents never really taught me much about money. They always tried to shield me from the emotional traumas that they went through when they had financial problems. I wish they had shared more of that with me, but they felt I should get as little of that as possible. They really didn't teach me how to handle money, either. If I ever wanted money, it was always there. I never had any experience at learning to manage money. Dad didn't give me an allowance, but always gave me all the money I asked for. Dad took care of all the money matters at home.

"Mark has been out of law school only three years, but he has done very well. I'm satisfied with the life which Mark has provided for me so far. I live in a nice house, drive a nice car, have pretty clothes, and have enough spending money to buy the things I like. I think our lifestyle will continue to improve because Mark is a very good lawyer. My job is to support him in everything he does, and I will be doing that as well as I can the next few years so that he will do the best he possibly can.

"We do have credit cards, but they are of no concern to me. Mark takes care of all those things. That's the way I want to live my life.

"Money doesn't really mean that much to me. I think there are lots of things that are more important than money. The most important thing is your family. Love is more important than money. You can have as much money as you want, but without being loved, the world is not going to be a warm place for you to live in. You could say the same thing about happiness. Being happy is more important to me than having a lot of money.

"Of course I'm thrilled Mark has done so well, because that has given me the same kind of security and freedom that I had with my father. Mark is a super provider, and knowing that we have plenty of money coming in takes the pressure off our marriage."

Although there are still some homemakers who "choose" Freda's monetary position as we enter the 1990s, times have really changed. Feminists have challenged and changed the money relationship between men and women, forever.

I recall a lecture given by anthropologist Margaret Mead in the 1950s, which I heard when I was a graduate student at NYU. She lectured on male and female roles in three South Pacific tribes. In one tribe, the men took care of the household while women hunted, fished, and farmed to bring home the food. She contrasted this group with tribes with male-female role definitions more similar to ours. Dr. Mead's point was obvious: Male and female roles can be culturally determined in any arrangement chosen.

Socially, women have been on the move to equalize their roles with men's, and they have succeeded to a great extent. It is now the norm for many women to be wage-earners. Women value economic independence, and it has been a primary focus of the women's movement. In a *Woman's Day* study (May 1987), of 60,000 of its readers, 92 percent of the sample, said it was a mistake to equate marriage with financial security. Women have learned the lesson of divorce—displaced homemakers—well; as Gloria Steinem said, "We are all one man away from welfare until we develop our earning power."

Women are collectively building up their financial identity. According to 1988 U.S. Census Bureau figures and New York Stock Exchange facts, women homeowners comprise 21 percent of the total homeowners nationwide, women own 24 percent of small businesses, and women are 50 percent of all stockholders.

What of women's earnings? While women still earn only 65 cents on every dollar a man earns, their salaries are rising, if disproportionately to men.

In the past two decades many women have gone from financial dependents to wage earners. Their right to earn is well established. Men and women now speak a new financial language, but is it the same language? In many ways, yes. As women have become fiscally fluent, they have come to feel the same positive money emotions that men feel. As men and women interact as financial equals, they also share a definite ambivalence about money as it relates to masculinity and to femininity. However, in one last area, *handling* money, many women are still novices. As a gender, many women are reluctant to master money issues head on. Dispelling this fear of money is the last challenge women face in their progressive quest for financial equality.

POSITIVE EMOTIONS ABOUT MONEY
WOMEN SHARE WITH MEN

In order to understand women's fear of money, let's first look at some of the positive emotions about money that women share with men.

Earning Money Feels Good

Men have always known that earning money feels good. Young boys are programmed to grow up to become good providers, breadwinners. A large part of becoming a man involves becoming a wage earner. A man who can not take care of his family, financially, is perceived as a failure. Making money in our culture "makes" the man. When a man is making "good" money, he feels good about himself.

Since women have joined the ranks of the working world, they too understand the good feelings attached to making money. Psychologists Rosalind Barnett and Grace Baruch of the Wellsley College Center for Research on Women studied women who work outside the home and have children, and women who have children but no paid-work role. Did the multiple roles of mother/wife/worker overstress women or were they beneficial? They found that being a mother, and not working, is associated with more depression and anxiety than any other role. A positive experience in a paid-work role can even offset some of the negative effects of being a mother. It may even enhance the relationship between a woman and her partner, because paid work gives women a sense of mastery. The happiest women of all were the ones working and raising families. Only women with low-paying, monotonous jobs didn't enjoy their multiple roles.

Lois Verbrugge of the University of Michigan, after studying health data based on thousands of women, came to a similar conclusion. She found that women who balanced career, marriage, and motherhood, regardless of age, were healthier than less involved women. A pay check, therefore, feels good to both men and women.

By contrast, the experience of women who have worked but have had to stop—for instance to have a child—can illustrate how bad it feels *not* to make money. In her article "The High Cost of Living Off Someone Else," in *Ms. Magazine*[1] Jane Lazone writes:

> During the three years when I stopped earning my own living, when I even stopped asking which bills were paid and which unpaid, when I was "supported" so that I might stay home and take care of my new baby, I used to spend a lot of time staring out the window. In my mind, or at times projected upon the huge, still buildings across the street, was the image of my stepmother, whom I had always admired, her finger pointing in my direction, her face wearing that expression she commonly uses when she knows she imparts the Truth: hard-won, unambivalent, eternal. "A woman," she says, "will never be free until she earns her own living."
>
> It is like a commandment from a new, feminine Jehovah, so absolute and inescapable does it seem to me. I close my weary eyes dreading the jungle of difficulties which awaits the next, inevitable step in my associations: Where will I work? Whom do I know? Who will keep the child? How much will *that* cost? I will take no job which will prevent me from being home by, say, three o'clock. And this "three o'clock" turns immediately into another rigid commandment, engraved in solid rock; coming home a minute after three means my baby will be a "latch-key kid," a lonely, deviant neurotic. . . .
>
> On many mornings, instead of trekking through this jungle once more, since I know I will end up in no sunny open pasture but instead go round and round until I fall asleep in the weeds, I just put it out of my mind. I *am* working, I say to myself, hurrying to the sink to wash the bottles. Then I separate the laundry, drag the vacuum out of the closet, stopping my continuous chores only long enough to rock the carriage furiously.

There is an excellent argument to be made for the position that women (or men) caring for young children are doing extremely valuable, if not always fascinating work. I believe this. But when I was doing this work to the exclusion of any other, I was never confident of my usefulness, and I rushed to erase the image of my stepmother which kept reappearing on the building wall. Now the reason for my lack of confidence is quite clear to me: I was not making any money.

I don't mean to idealize paid labor. Clearly, most jobs in this society are characterized by both financial and psychological exploitation. But the financial and psychological ramifications of *not* working for a living, as well as the idealization of this way of life for women and young children, must be understood on their own terms. There is a special kind of stupefaction and infantilizing that erodes the confidence and sometimes the abilities of those who derive the supposed benefits of being supported by another. Social myth notwithstanding, most people are forced to be supported—like older people, sick people, teenagers and many wives—don't like it and are quick to say so.[2]

Once women taste self-sufficiency and fiscal independence, it's often ego-shattering to go back to that old dependent role. Earning money is tied to one's sense of personal worth.

Earning Money Feels Sexy

Masculinity has long been defined in terms of power, money, and dominance. Money equals success and sexiness. Both sexes agree that financial success is an aphrodisiac. It's not surprising that many men buy into this myth and connect potency with income. When the income plummets, in some cases so does potency.

Psychologists Paul Frish and Ann Frish carried out an interesting study of the relationship between sexual performance and money (reported in *The New York Times*, November 23, 1986). They investigated the behavior of thirty males involved in the stock market, either as investors or as Wall Street employees. When the market went up, so did the sex drive of these men [who were in counseling for non-sexual problems]. When the market went down, there was a high incidence of sexual problems.[3] This correlation between sexual surges and the Dow Jones industrial average reflects both on the men and on their sexual partners. A man's sense of potency was related to his fiscal performance and so was his partner's response to him, telling him indirectly his attractiveness was relative to his scoring on the market.

Many of my male clients over the years have related their virility to money. One of my clients, a man of thirty-six who was inhibited and socially inept, was sure that no woman would find him attractive unless he was making a lot of money or had the appropriate toys of affluence. He had been raised in a strict religious home, and had had limited contact with girls and no dating experience until his second year of college. During his treatment it became evident that he was painfully insecure about his abilities in any area. Money was his "cover": if he flashed a roll of bills, no one would see how little else there was to him. He needed expensive clothes, a big sporty car, and thick wallet, and he had a large gun collection—all extensions of his genitals. He believed money would get him beautiful girls because it would show he could give them what they needed.

Many therapists concur that both sexes are responsible for the perpetration of this money/virility myth. Both genders too often "say" the size of a man's income is somehow equated to the size of his penis. Some women aggrandize men who are ordinary except for their bank accounts. In general, rich men are a turn-on, poor ones a turn-off. In this social/sexual/monetary context, men are overly affected. The effects can range from low interest in sex during difficult financial times to extremes of sexual impotence in the face of disastrous business ventures, as countless cases have proven.

The effect of money-making on virility is often subtle, but not always. In my research, men reported feeling more daring in their relationships when they were doing well financially. This was sharply etched in the sexual patterns of gamblers, for example. One gambler's comment summed up the finding. "When I'm doing good at the track, I'm always more interested in women. When I'm a loser I want to lock myself away in a cave and not see anyone, especially a woman."

Whether resulting from a day at the races or daily experiences in the rat race, many men report feeling exceptionally sexual immediately following financial successes in their lives.

Women do not just conspire in this money-makes-men-sexy myth. Now they too experience firsthand the feeling that earning feels sexy.

Some research reveals that career women have better sex lives than homemakers and noncareerists. Although career women may find it harder to schedule lovemaking because of their busy schedules, they report more sexual joy when they have sex than homemakers do.

Women do apparently feel sexier when they are making money, but do men find them sexier as breadwinners? That is ultimately the question—and the rub and the bad news in all this good news about working women feeling better and sexier.

Being a good provider is crucial for a man, a definite plus, almost the hinge of a good relationship and self-image. Being a good provider is hardly that simple for a woman. Is her career good for her family, her marriage, her femininity? Men and women share an ambivalence in answering these questions.

DOES WORKING WORK AGAINST WOMEN — AND THEIR RELATIONSHIPS WITH MEN?

First, consider the question itself. Men have never faced a similar innuendo. Most working men with hard-driving careers are congratulated, not implicated in strained marriages, neglectful child-rearing, or the ego destruction of their mates. It is only women who go off to work with an added burden of guilt and a vague unease that their working is at their family's expense. If a successful male cuts his office time to spend more time with his young children, it is a matter of choice, not pressure. Today's women are under the cultural gun to have it all—job, man, kids—and do it all, simultaneously feeling their lot is impossible.

While working hard has become a legitimate part of the feminine ethic, making big bucks has not. Women's fear of success, documented by experts and admittedly felt by thousands of women, has been exposed and somewhat overcome. Women go after achievement, accomplishment, with gusto, societal approval, and even mate's applause. However, when it comes to the paycheck that goes along with that level of success, a new fear is brewing for women and men: the fear of wealth, women's wealth.

Many men and women resist, recoil, and react negatively to feminine earning power. From a man's viewpoint, what could be so bad about spending your wife's money? Having a double income, double spending power? It's being *shown up* as a breadwinner that men can find diminishing.

Bill's case makes this point. He was caught in a bind. A successful doctor, he divided his time between research, which he found enjoyable but not very rewarding financially, and the practice of internal medicine, which was lucrative but not so enjoyable. He felt it a strain to deal with many diverse people and was more comfortable with animal research, which also fulfilled his creative talents and led to his writing a number of solid scientific papers. Bill's wife, Maria, an actress who had only middling success, became an actors' agent and clicked right away.

Soon Maria began to earn more money than Bill. At first he joked about it with her and even with close friends, but, as it turned out later, the joking was uneasy, and laden with anxiety. Bill decided to increase his patient practice at the expense of his research. He forced himself to make more money—when he actually needed less, thanks to Maria's high income.

They began quarreling about many small things—arguments without resolutions because they had nothing to do with the real issue: that her new moneymaking powers were a threat to his masculinity.

Bill and Maria went into therapy because they were considering separating after eight years of a happy marriage. After a number of sessions, it became clear that Bill felt Maria's success meant she didn't need him anymore, that he had been diminished as "the man of the house." This was not easy for him to admit; he had always claimed he was happy to see his wife doing what she wanted to professionally. But this was the first time he had to face her actually succeeding at it. Bill agreed, with some ambivalence, to go into therapy. As his therapy evolved, his problem with "masculinity" emerged even more clearly. He had never felt comfortable competing with men; this was a contributing factor to his going into research. He really received very little gratification from his medical practice, but he needed to make a lot of money to feel competent as a man.

Men like Bill feel financially cuckolded, even emasculated, by a wife's earnings, even though they are supposed to be liberated. When a

3 5

wife puts her money where her husband's liberated mouth is, he's often in trouble emotionally. The man who, like the breadwinners of the 50s, still blatantly states the macho-man position that "no wife of mine needs to work" (an update of the old "no wife of mine will ever work") may have fewer conflicts than the "liberated" man who, like Bill, espouses equality yet harbors macho feelings on an unconscious level.

Many women pick up the theme that men feel threatened by their earning power. It does more than take the air out of their professional balloons; it adds to old fears they already have about femininity and money. For example, "If I earn like a man, will he see me as less of a woman?" Or "By earning money like a man, am I betraying some womanly heritage? Even 'spitting in the eye' of my mother, who never stooped to financial dealings? Voices such as these accost women who make good money, bringing into question their own femininity, scratching at the surface of deep psychic conflicts they have over leading lives so opposite from those lived by their mothers.

Psychological mixed messages which push women forward into the new fiscal frontier and simultaneously pull them back give many women this fear of feminine wealth. The next case, reported by Vivian Gornick in *The Village Voice,* tells of one woman whose wealth carried a price tag of several problems. She tried to just block the entire confounding, confusing, issue of money from her mind.

> For many years, while David worked steadily and was a bulwark of emotional stability, Joyce stayed home, gave birth to and raised the children, and was a very nervous lady—strained, restless, sometimes verging on hysteria. So great in fact was Joyce's nervousness that her super intelligence was forgotten: by both Joyce and David, as well as most of their friends and relatives. It was commonly assumed that Joyce was emotionally frail, and that was what made the marriage so beautiful, so tender, the combination of Joyce's frailty and David's protectiveness.
>
> Then Joyce entered law school. She went through the three-year course like lightning, graduated high in her class, and passed the bar exam first time out. Who could figure out what happened? All of a sudden the cobwebs cleared out of her mind, the nervousness disappeared; she worked, she studied, she did brilliantly. And her marriage very nearly fell apart.
>
> The tension in their house became unbearable, exploding four nights a week into bitter quarrels. They survived this. They both loved their children very much, and their home, and they wanted to stay

married. So they "worked" at it. In certain ways they even flourished. Joyce got a fine job in a good law firm and within a short time she was doing very well, both loving her work and bringing home a great deal of money. In fact, very quickly she was earning more money than David, whose job teaching history at a community college had always gained him only a modest income. They moved into a spacious apartment in a better section of the city, bought beautiful furniture, and sent their children to private schools and expensive summer camps.

In other ways Joyce seemed to flourish too. Her politics had always been very liberal, on occasion radical. The work she was doing allowed her to take many pro bono cases as well as perform many legal services for the neighborhood community. Her parents were proud of her: Here she was doing well, and she had not forgotten where she came from.

One evening Joyce and I had dinner. An application form of some sort was tossed on top of her desk, and surrounding it were many sheets of yellow legal-size paper covered with columns of figures, scratched out, rewritten, altogether unintelligible. Joyce followed my glance, "That's a grant application I'm trying to fill out. It requires my listing all the sources of my income and I'm going crazy trying to do it. I don't know what my income is."

Joyce sank into a chair, looking suddenly, strangely distracted. For a moment she seemed to have difficulty speaking. Then she blurted, "That's exactly what I mean. I don't know. I've never known. I don't really know how much I bring in. I just bring home the paycheck, sign it, and turn it over to David. And any other monies I get, I do the same."

"I have never, never felt at ease with making money." The implication of her gaze was obvious. It was mainly her income that kept this establishment afloat. "I know it's mainly my money that provides us with the life we lead. And yet, it seems, somehow, impossible for me to take direct responsibility for it. I feel *guilty* for wanting money, *guilty* for making it, *guilty* toward David, *guilty* toward my parents, *guilty* toward other women, *guilty* toward every single person in this lousy society who can't make enough money."[4]

There are at least three money/femininity issues here: (1) The fact that David is a closet macho and has difficulty handling his wife's affluence, hence Joyce's wifely guilts; (2) The fact that Joyce is uncomfortable with the whole money subject, from wanting to earning, hence her anxiety; and (3) —an added twist due to feminist identity—the fact that Joyce feels as if getting rich has betrayed some feminine pact with underprivileged people.

How rich can a woman become without feeling guilty? Joyce's guilt is felt by many of today's compassionate, sensitive, successful people, but especially by women. Having always identified with the powerless female underclass, they wake up one day to find themselves in the rich camp. They subsequently feel guilty for having power, money, and privilege in a world where so many women have naught. A subliminal, subtle sense of distress leads to an ostrich-like reaction to their finances.

Joyce's economic success put her feminist history, her female identity, her marriage, her husband's sense of competence—all these on the line. Is it any wonder she opted for a kind of ostrich stance, refusing to learn anything about her own finances?

Add to these money guilts the implication that she's neglecting latch-key children or aging parents, or insulting her mother's plight psychologically, and you have some idea of what women are up against vis à vis feminine wealth. Women are damned if they own up to their accumulated wealth, destined to tunnel through the conflicts in order to bask in the psychic rewards. Yet they are also damned if they take that ostrich dive.

THE GRIM LESSONS OF FINANCIAL DEPENDENCE

Every woman has heard stories about divorce, single parenting, homelessness, and widowhood, stories with the lethal Catch-22 lesson: If you can't depend on yourself financially, you're doomed. One older woman I interviewed, Marlene, a seventy-three-year-old widow, laments her problems: "I don't know what I'm going to do. I never worked because Clint took care of my money problems. He was a good provider. Since he died three years ago I've been living off the government and what little money we had put away. Now that money is almost gone.

"I'm really stuck, because there is no way I can make money. I have been active in organizations all my life, but none of them will give me a job. If I want to volunteer my time, it's okay, but if I need to get paid, it's not okay. You could say I'm disillusioned by my whole life.

"I think about money all the time. It's always in the front of my brain because I always have some bill hanging over my head. I spend most of my time managing my money, because if I make mistakes I don't have enough to eat decently on. I never really had a hand in managing the money when Clint was alive. He'd give me an allowance, and that was about it. I didn't have to worry about paying the bills. All I ever did was buy groceries. I didn't even know how much money we had put away.

"Now I wish that Clint had given me a chance to work with him on money management. It would have saved me a lot of trouble in the long run. We never talked about money, though. Clint always felt he had to shield me from those things, and he did a great job. Only now I'm the big loser. I don't feel sorry for myself. I just wish that Clint had let me in on some of this so that I didn't get such a big surprise when he passed away.

"I thought we would have put more money away than we did. I don't know what to do or who to turn to. I've tried everything I know and there is no way out.

"I used to think a lot of things were more important than money. I don't anymore. If you would have asked me five years ago, I would have told you that love, happiness, and health were more important. I always believed that until I saw what happens to a person when they don't have enough money to pay their bills or do the things they have to do.

"Money is the only thing that can buy security. Late at night, I sit and shake because I'm afraid I'm going to get robbed or mugged. This used to be a nice area; now it's dangerous to live here.

"In the old days I would never consider hurting anybody or doing anything wrong for money. But now that I've had to starve to stay alive, I would do just about anything you asked.

"I don't really know what the value of credit is. I can't get credit anywhere, and I can't scrape up enough cash to do the job that needs to be done at home. Clint didn't like credit. The only thing that we bought that we didn't pay cash for was our house. I don't even know how much the payments were, only that Clint always used to complain about how high they were. Still, he managed to pay them on time. He was a man who kept his word.

"Me, I'm going to spend the rest of my days in poverty. I've read enough Agatha Christie books to think I could get away with murder if

I planned it meticulously enough. For a million dollars I would kill anybody."

It's a grim tale, a terrified woman plotting a murder that will never take place, all because of a status quo of fiscal incompetence, money blindness—and it mirrors the plight of an entire generation of elderly women. Today's women hear these stories and know they must heed the lessons well. But how? They have a lot to overcome.

Ambivalence about female earning power (and money management is articulated emotionally by both sexes, and it has thoroughly sabotaged women. Women's psyches have been manhandled by mixed messages and a double dose of fear—fear of becoming rich and fear of becoming poor.

SELF-SABOTAGING ATTITUDES

My research revealed a clear pattern of difference between the sexes in their concepts of their own fiscal competence. More men than expected statistically and fewer women than expected statistically felt they handled money sensibly. The younger the women in my research, the more foolish they felt in their economic management, with teen-age girls feeling most foolish. We can conclude that women feel that they do not handle money sensibly.

New York psychologist Annette Lieberman studied the financial attitudes and behaviors of 125 women for her 1987 book with Vicki Lindner, *Unbalanced Accounts: Why Women Are Still Afraid of Money.* She found the majority of women in her study had not learned how to handle—or even thought about handling—their money despite how important money was to their well-being. She reported that the nature of a woman's relationship to money significantly added to or detracted from her feelings of control over her life, her self-esteem, her sense of freedom and security. Women failed basic competency in money skills because of a variety of phobias, according to Lieberman, ranging from money folly, money squeamishness, and money paranoia to money denial and money eluding.

Lieberman found many examples of women mishandling their

economic business, and of self-sabotaging attitudes and postures as well. She notes in one case of a lady named Julia that women are waking up to their money problems. Julia comments: "I was taught that wanting money was greedy and bad, somehow not 'high-minded' enough. I'm still resentful that nobody taught me—ever—how important money was. I know now money sets you free."[5]

Now that the issues of financial responsibility, money phobias, and fiscal competence are being brought to the attention of a female audience, women are recognizing monetary behaviors that are not in their best interests. For example, the compulsive shopper syndrome has received much attention. Women are now keenly aware of their penchant to spend money emotionally to assuage emotional pain related to other aspects of their lives.

In my research I found several other female economic postures that were more subtle, less well-documented, but no less sabotaging. Financial drifting and financial dreaming are perhaps the most prevalent.

Sally's story is relevant. A part-time student, Sally works as an assistant manager at a Taco Bell fast food stand, lives at home with her parents, and at age nineteen said: "My parents still help support me. That will go on, they keep telling me, until I catch the right guy. I feel my father sees me as a financial burden that will only let up when I get married off. Most of my girlfriends just hang out waiting for a guy to take care of them.

"Even though I'm working, I don't see money as a big deal in my life. My father owns a liquor store and I can usually get any money I want off him. Also when I date, I have no money worries. It's a matter of picking guys who take me where I want to go."

It's obvious from Sally's lackadaisical attitude toward financial matters, fiscal independence is not on her mind or agenda. Even in the postfeminist era there are still many unenlightened young women like Sally who will just lead their lives drifting from financial dependence on their fathers to financial dependence on their husbands. The modern twist to this is that living in the 90s now requires two incomes, and women like Sally may well have to work at Taco Bells way past marriage unless they cultivate skills that will afford better working options.

It's not surprising to find financial drifters in the lower rungs of the social ladder, where feminism, ambition, and progressive independence have not made substantial inroads into women's thoughts. However, it is surprising to see drifters in middle income women. For women like Carol, twenty-nine, single, a teacher, financial independence is sought and acquired but only in a temporary framework. The future is still left adrift. She said: "My parents always tried to make me money-conscious. When I was four, they gave me my first piggybank. My father would usually drop a coin or two in there when he got home from work. They thought it would teach me how to save, but I don't think it worked too well.

"I've been working as a teacher for nearly seven years now. I haven't managed to save a penny. I have been able to pile up some pretty impressive debts, though, which really have my parents distressed. They can't understand how anybody who makes as much as I do, with so few obligations, could have financial difficulties.

"My parents have put a great deal of pressure on me to be financially successful, but I still have to borrow every now and then from them to pay my bills. I like to travel and I take off every summer. So far I've been to Europe three times, the Caribbean, the Orient, and I've taken two trips to Central America and Mexico and one around the United States. I have a tremendous desire to travel. I think I got the travel bug from my parents, who always wanted to go but never took the plunge. I'm living out some of their travel fantasies and it costs a lot.

"I have always found guys with money to be more attractive to me, just because they could take me places that had class. I like fancy restaurants and I like nice things. It takes money to afford me.

"There are some things that are more important than money. I would rank independence higher than money. I'm not a women's libber, but I'm going to hold out as long as I can as far as marrying a guy for money. I never want to fall into the trap of being dependent on him for my sustenance."

Carol is kidding herself. She works, yes, but she is hardly financially independent in the broad sense. Her financial independence is illusory, still grounded in the knowledge that she can hit her parents for money when necessary. Her goals are fiscally immature because they are only present-oriented, and are focused primarily on recreation. What of long-range priorities? Carol's not saving to accumulate holdings or to make purchases like a home. She is just letting the future take care of itself. Implied by this posture is the assumption that some man will come along and plan the future for her. Even though she bristles at becoming dependent on a man, who else will bail her out financially or chart her course if and when her parents bow out? If she doesn't take full fiscal responsibility for her future by beginning to plan now, she'll have to be beholden to someone else.

Carol is adrift in the present, which is a common economic condition among today's single professional women. They work, earn, and spend it all on today's necessities or luxuries with little, if any, eye on the future. They avoid financial commitments like home owning, dismiss moves to accumulate a financial nest egg, almost as if planning the future without a man would somehow jinx the odds that there will be a man to plan that elusive future for them or with them.

Financial drifting is not just a woman's trap, to be sure. And the high cost of living in the 80s and 90s has trapped many young people at home, depriving them of the chance to get their feet wet in real households of their own economic making. Yet financial drifting is especially dangerous for women because they need that long-range picture and experience if they intend to become truly self-sufficient permanently, not just temporarily. It requires forethought, planning, daring to take on the future alone so that if a man comes along, he will be an added bonus, not a financial lifeline.

Another sabotaging financial posture is financial dreaming. This can not only afflict the financially dependent woman, but also the woman who intends to make her own way financially in the world but lacks the specifics of a plan. Her focus is not on skill-building. It is not on setting up a five-year plan professionally and proceeding step by step. Her fiscal philosophy is abstract, almost magical.

Jennifer, twenty-six, is a dance instructor who hates her job and is trying to succeed by concentrating on her karma, her mental energies. "I'm doing this dance instructor job for one reason—the money. I hate my work and just about everything else in my life right now. I am totally unhappy with the amount of money I have. I think of myself as a failure right now, but as my life improves, I'm sure I'll see myself in a better light.

"I would rather be rich than anything else in the world. I have money on the brain. I think about it all the time. I've read a lot of motivational books and they all say if you want to make money badly enough, that you will [have it] some day. I've been using positive thinking for about five years now, but nothing has really happened."

Daydreaming financially may well be a psychic aid to success, but without a realistic roadmap it will not lead to miraculous millions. Both women and men fall into this trap, but women are at greater risk because they have less financial training to rely on. Dreaming needs reality to back it up.

Jennifer is coming around to realizing that lately. As she said, "I have always been enthralled with poetry. I've decided I want a chance to teach high school kids about it. I want to be an English teacher."

Now with a plan, a college enrollment, and a set goal, Jennifer's money dream has more chance of becoming a reality.

Women have come a long way from financial dependence to economic independence. By building financial sense along with marketable skills they have become earners, some even big earners. The next step is acquiring a fiscal perspective and the economic skills to guarantee a successful future in addition to a successful present.

Finance is a language most men were taught from birth. Women must learn to speak it fluently, too. When it comes right down to money talk, women and men do understand one another. They do speak the same financial language when it comes to what money delivers, and even when it comes to comprehending how money threatens their masculinity and femininity. They speak a common, if not simple, tongue complete with ambivalences which both understand. Women have cashed in on feelings of worth. Their remaining challenge is to discount the ambivalent dialect (along with men), manage their fears about money, and master the vocabulary of handling their hard won assets.

4

Marriage and Money

ONE PHONY, but popular, myth about the role of money and caring in marriage is demonstrated in the TV advertisement which shows a well-dressed married couple in formal attire, ascending to their room in an elevator, in a luxury hotel after an apparently wonderful night on the town. The wife appears to be distant until her husband surprises her with the diamond ring he has bought for their wedding anniversary. They then float into their bedroom to an obviously romantic ending for the evening. The screen is lit with the admonition, "A diamond shows you still care." This advertiser's viewpoint reveals only one small element related to money in marriage.

Money is a potent force in most marriages, and oftentimes an explosive one. At the outset, you are dealing with two people, each with his or her own money style, history, and emotions. Putting them together to run one household too often translates into pitting them against each other. Money often becomes the battlefield of conflicting emotions, some directly related to money matters, and others to conflicts in the sexual and emotional security arena. In my study, 72 percent of my married respondents indicated they have conflict and fight over money.

Doctors Pepper Schwartz and Philip Blumstein summed up marital monetary history in their book, *American Couples.* "In study after study, going back several decades, between one-quarter and one-third of all married couples ranked money as their primary problem."[1]

The issue of money and marriage is even more relevant as we begin the 1990s because of two-career marriages. Dr. David H. Olsen, professor of family social science at the University of Minnesota, surveyed 5285 couples and found one of the most significant marital flashpoints is "power struggles emerging over money."[2]

My research suggests that several factors exacerbate the conflict; for example, education. An inverse relationship seems to exist between the educational level of the spouses and the frequency of money fights. People with less than a high school education are apt to "often" argue over money, while those with college degrees are much less likely to argue over money. Perhaps this is because those with higher education are apt to have better jobs and more money and thus less reason to bicker. We can also speculate that education per se may make some people more effective in handling money and thus less inclined to fight. Further, people with more education may be better integrated into society and generally have fewer negative emotional issues impinging upon their lives, whereas those with less education are more apt to be poor and struggling with their daily existence, so that money becomes the battleground for fighting over many other issues.

Although it was no great surprise to prove that couples with less education are more apt to fight over money, it was a surprise to see the significant relationship between age and the degree of money battles within marriages. In the forty-something age bracket, fewer individuals are found who say they "never fight" over money than expected, and more who say they "fight constantly" over money with their spouse than expected. When couples turn fifty, the odds on money harmony change. More people than expected aged fifty plus say they "never fight" over money with their spouse. Perhaps by this time, if the couple is still together, they have resolved the issue.

I would speculate that forty is a crisis age, and money becomes a battleground for other problems in a married couple's life at that time. During the forties it becomes increasingly more difficult to hold onto jobs against the flood of younger competition; hence, midlife paranoia can surface. This is also the age when many people are putting their children through college, a modern financial feat, and taking on some responsibility for longer-living, aged parents. The forties can be the time when "the sandwich generation" feels most squeezed economically as well as emotionally. Divorce rates are higher as people go through a passage, a change of life, and marriages risk going stale. People looking for an argument at age forty can find lots of issues to confront in money matters.

If people are able to weather the tides of forty, perhaps that is why at fifty, fighting over money slows down. My sample had a higher than average yearly income, so many fifty-plus people tended to be retirees with financial security factored into their lives.

CLASHING MONEY STYLES

The relationship of age and education to money battles makes a crucial statement about how money affects marriage, as does tying income and education level to fighting frequency. Just as an individual's money style is central to his or her individual well-being, a couple's compatible or incompatible money styles are central to the harmony in their relationship. There appear to be two main patterns of conflict over money within marriage: overt differences, stemming from clashing money styles and spending habits; and covert differences, stemming from hidden agendas behind money styles. Money battles are, therefore, often symbolic of deeper conflicts.

The story of Larry, a writer, and his homemaker wife, Diane, illustrates both patterns of conflict. Larry could be categorized as Contented in terms of money styles, and Diane as Insatiable. Their own words from a taped interview show how money battles emerge and how deep they run.

Larry began, "My financial situation is quite beyond anything I'd ever hoped for. I feel I'm living extremely well. I have a nice car, a valuable home, and a good income. Yet I feel that, rightly or wrongly, my wife still thinks I'm a financial failure as a husband. She's always whining about what she doesn't have. I feel there are literally millions of women who would be delighted and content to live at our financial level, yet she constantly complains. I feel that I've failed as a husband, failed as a man. Personally, I think I have everything I want, I'm living far beyond my wildest expectations, but my wife is still dissatisfied!"

Now, Diane's side: "I identify with my peers and according to them I'm not doing well. I'm married to a supposedly successful man and my friends live better than I do. I go into their homes and they've got their houses together pretty well. I mean, there are sofas in the living room. There's an old couch in my living room! I almost left Larry over one tiny Oriental rug. My friend was selling one cheap and I brought it home for him to take a look at it. He went nuts, calling me names out on the front lawn, no less! He was yelling all over the damn neighborhood. I left for a while, then I changed my mind.

"Larry's the kind of person that unless it just falls in our laps, he will not aggressively go out to look to make more money for any furniture or anything. If it was up to him we wouldn't get anything. One day I said something about a piano. It would be good for our son to learn piano. I'd like to play piano because my mother played it. He said, 'No piano,' and off he went again on and on about the rug."

To me, it's clear that Larry and Diane are caught in a game of clashing financial interests. Larry's money style is Contented; he set goals logically and has achieved them and more. He is very pleased with his accomplishments and the lifestyle they deliver. His only source of displeasure and bone of contention is his wife's response. Diane is an Insatiable, summed up in this comment of hers: "I don't want to play any games. At forty years old I just want my house to get done and then I can move on to something else. A bigger house? Of course!"

Opposite money styles mean trouble in marriage. It can happen at any level of the socioeconomic ladder. Doctors Pepper Schwartz and Phillip Blumstein report, after reading 12,000 questionnaires and conducting 300 in-depth follow-up interviews for their book *American Couples,* that couples argue about how money is managed more than about how much they have—and this finding held true across all income levels.[3]

How money is doled out and managed by a Contented versus an Insatiable presents a difference of opinion destined to clash. From the simplest choice, such as buying a car, to the broadest choices involved in defining a lifestyle, their opposite orientations spell "arguments." The Contented person opts for the Chevrolet and is happy to have it. The Insatiable person desperately *needs* the Mercedes that they can't afford; and when they get it they *need* a Rolls Royce. Each could be happy with his/her choice; neither can be happy when one wins at the other's expense.

Family History

As complicated as coupling two spouses with different money styles can be, even more complex is the covert theme running beneath the surface of mundane money squabbles. This becomes clear as Larry and Diane go on bickering into deeper psychological territory.

Larry said, "I'd like to present my point of view. I would like to have a little financial cushion because I have had the stark terror of seeing my father out of work during the Depression. He couldn't get a job. Not that we were totally broke, we were eating, but I could see his face. He'd sit home all day. I probably have, deep down, a strong fear of being in a position like that.

"When my wife sees the weeds coming up in front on the lawn, she's plunged into the emotions of being back in the trailer camp where she grew up. I understand her financial terror. She's living in a $500,000 home, but when she sees those weeds she thinks she's back in that camp, and indigent."

Diane concurred. "I have a feeling of well-being when the grass is mowed and there's some order. Our lawn was the disgrace of the neighborhood. I cried and Larry finally called a guy to come and dig out the weeds. I'm forty years old and today for the first time I have a gardener!

"I don't like disorder and I don't like filth. It reminds me of a bunch of Okies—people who don't give a shit about themselves or anything around them. Have you ever gone to these kinds of Okie places? There's always some hulks of cars rusting out, and weeds."

In the final analysis, there are deeper fears compelling each spouse to fight for their money rights. Larry's afraid of going broke like his father did; he's scarred by childhood memories. Diane is terrified of living like her parents did—Okie-style—and determined to erase the tiniest resemblance to her past. She's driven to keep moving up to better houses, with better furnishings, up and *away* from her memories.

Issues like fear and self-esteem are murky; certainly less clear than furniture preferences. Yet the choice of home furnishings represents unconscious ripples, which clash and complicate money encounters between spouses. Each spouse's family history, where money styles originate, provides clues to unravel economic stalemates like Larry and Diane's.

Incompatibility

In my research I asked, "If you are married, do you (or if you are divorced, did you) and your spouse share the same views on money?" Thirty-eight percent claimed they did *not* share the same view. Sixty-two percent believed they shared similar views, but upon closer scrutiny disagreement appeared there too. More married men believed their views were dissonant with their wives; married women more often seemed to believe their views were in accord with their husbands. Were women fooling themselves because they felt guilty about their spending? Were men biased to be contrary? Although viewpoint discrepancies are hard to pinpoint, what's perfectly obvious is that money viewpoints are rarely understood, much less communicated effectively and harmoniously.

When people with opposing viewpoints about money marry each other, you usually wind up with an incompatible couple, as demonstrated by the case of Jack and Marta.

Jack saw things like this: "Now that I'm fairly well-established in my profession, I feel money has let me change my opinion on certain issues. I find people have more confidence in me because I've made money. Professionally, money's made me more inclined to give more time to the clients paying the most. I'd always pick the highest-paying job over job fulfillment, something I never believed I'd do. If you asked me that as a student, the challenge was the more important things. The funny thing now is, the more money I earn, the more of a challenge I find it to make more than last year!

"My interpersonal relationships have changed, but not too much. I'm basically a loner, so seeking friendships is not a problem. I can see through people. I can tell if they are interested in me or my money.

"Marta and I do argue more. I guess it does stem from the issue of money. Money does cause evil in me, but I couldn't be happy without it. My dad was a businessman involved with big transactions. He once showed me a large check and told me all that I could buy with it. I guess he had a profound effect on me, because I have never forgotten that scene.

"Is it deviant to want a big house, nice cars and clothes, and to go to the Club whenever possible? As my holdings rise, I'll keep a close eye on developments because I want to keep moving up in the world. Money is important to me and it seems like the more I get, the more I want."

Marta's main gripe was that Jack was not the man she married anymore. "Since Jack made it financially, he is a different person, not always for the better. He has become callous in his dealings with people, and more hostile. This coldness carries over into our marriage. He used to be kind and gentle. But I guess you can't be out there beating people for all the money you can and then come home at night and turn it right off. He's changed since we've become rich.

"My dissatisfaction with our life together has come because of his high earning power. Our relationship has been altered because of his hardened personality and my reaction to the new Jack. When I worked, the money was ours, but now that he is doing well, getting money from him is impossible. Money is his driving force. People, including me, are secondary. I don't know how much longer I will be able to take it. His money drive is killing our marriage."

Jack is a classic Insatiable, hard-driving, obsessive about earning money, and not satisfied no matter how high his net worth goes. He views money as central to his ego, his purpose in life, and has early family memories which laid the foundation for this money perspective. Marta says he's changed, but chances are he's only blossomed in his

51

view. To her way of thinking, he's become corrupt. To Marta, money is simply not as important as tenderness, marriage, free time—things low on Jack's personal agenda. She would have been content with far less; he'll never be content.

Jack and Marta have incompatible money styles, and this affects their priorities. In this case, one person's fantasy—becoming rich—is the other's nightmare. In this case, their marital strife surrounding money is following a course quite common, according to my observations of couples in therapy with me who are dissonant in terms of money styles. I found many relationships go from denial of the importance of money during courtship, to arguments over money during marriage, to an attempt to destroy each other during divorce.

Whether Jack and Marta would let their marriage deteriorate to a contested divorce was unclear. However, had they known and understood each other's views on money at the start, they could have been saved mutual disillusionment.

Attitudes about money are really a statement of personal values expressed in a person's money style. When personal values are dissonant, money styles are incompatible. Couples in this conflict situation often lose respect for one another.

When Paul's idealism clashed with Vera's materialism, the only solution was dissolving their marriage. Paul was a show business lawyer. He met Vera when she consulted him about a legal problem she was having with a theatrical agency. She had a degree in theater arts, and was moderately successful doing commercials, aiming at a serious acting career.

Paul remembered, "When I first met her, Vera literally floored me. I was thirty-five, she was twenty. She was the most gorgeous woman I had ever seen in my life. That first year was pure heaven. We were in love. We'd go to bed on Friday night and wake up Sunday night. When she became pregnant, there was no question. I wanted to marry her and have our child.

"After we married, there was no real thought about any other woman. And remember, in my business I deal with beautiful women and many of them were very sexually available. Sure I was tempted, but I took my marriage vows seriously and I was very committed to Vera and the baby.

"We had one conflict that we could never resolve. It related to materialism: She was; I wasn't. She wanted the whole Hollywood trip— the house in Beverly Hills, the Mercedes, all of it. She was money-oriented and I have never been. I really wanted the opposite. I hated all the phoniness of Hollywood wheeling and dealing. In law school I was a purist and really into jurisprudence. Philosophy of law was my interest. I was leaning toward what I felt would be a more honest way of life before Vera came along. I wanted to be a professor of law.

"I was teaching part-time at a law school and shooting for a full-time position. Vera's materialism killed that off at the time. She wanted me to earn more and more. With a wife like that and a kid, teaching was out of the question.

"That was our tug of war all the time that my daughter was growing up. Vera's hunger for more money and success, my struggle to teach law and lead an intellectual life. One day I decided for me it was now or never. My midlife crisis or male menopause? I quit all of the Hollywood bullshit and took a position at the university. My pay was cut in half. That did it. Vera and I were at each other's throats.

"We went separate ways. Vera tried to resume her career, but a thirty-six-year-old actress is in a tough spot. We began to look outside of our marriage for friends and lovers for the first time in our lives."

The conflict in a marriage like this, when one person is materialistic and the other is not, develops because the materialist demands too much and spends too much. Paul said, "During our marriage Vera spent around 80 percent of our income on things she wanted and I hated! You can imagine our battles over money."

Paul could not live out his values, fulfill his goals of idealism and the intellectual life, and feel personally contented so long as he stayed linked to Vera's Insatiable traits. Their divorce decree was written, inevitably, in irreconcilable values and money styles.

"I've been divorced for two years now and my wife's alimony meter keeps running. When we were married for fifteen years, I earned all of the money. She was a shopaholic and spent 80 percent of my income on fashionable crap. On the order of the courts, I'm still paying. My marriage was like a war that I lost. In my divorce, after the war, as the loser I was forced to pay the victor war reparations."

HIDDEN AGENDAS—BALANCE OF
POWER

Not all money battles stem from clashing money styles. Sometimes a couple can have compatible styles, viewpoints, and values, and yet have fiscal fireworks. Covert money issues, hidden money agendas, infect countless marriages and intimate relationships. Money becomes the battleground, but peace can only reign when the secret agenda is uncovered.

Charles and Lisa are a very affluent married couple, living in a fashionable neighborhood in Connecticut. He is a doctor. Lisa doesn't have to, or want to, work. They are both contented, satisfied with their lives and lifestyle. That doesn't mean they haven't fought over money; they have. However, as you listen to them reveal how they solved their running argument over Lisa's spending habits, you will see the real issue wasn't money at all.

Lisa somewhat proudly confessed, "Four years ago I started paying the bills. Charles always paid the bills before that. He was in charge of the money. Now I pay them, and I don't have to ask him for money. I don't have to account to him for what I buy. I know how much we have. I feel I can judge as well as he can whether or not we can afford something. I've taken that responsibility *not* to buy.

"Sometimes I might feel like I am splurging. But generally, when I buy something I feel okay about it. When Charles controlled the money, I often used money as a weapon against him. You know, when I got mad at him, I'd go out and buy something expensive. To hell with him, I'm going to buy this purse or that dress!"

How could Charles turn over all the money responsibility to a wife he believed was a shopaholic? Insight made him do it. As he explained, "I'm glad I let her take over the paying of the bills because it's resolved our money conflicts. When I paid the bills, I'd find out that we didn't have the money for all these bills. I'd question, Where's the money going? Lisa had a checkbook for small bills and pocket money. I'd look through her checkbook and see this store and that store. I'd get angry and yell at her for spending all the money. We'd sit down and try to figure it out. Somehow we could never really figure it out.

"Once we were in a group session for married couples. Someone asked me, 'How do you handle your money?' I reported I was giving my wife an allowance, and she would always spend it, whatever it was. Somebody in the group said, 'That's stupid. Why don't you let her write the checks and handle the money? Don't you work hard enough?' I said I didn't like that idea. 'Why not?' I started thinking about it. My fear was that if I turned the money over to her, we would be turned into paupers in no time flat! Also, I later determined that turning this task over to her messed with my macho image of what a 'real' man does. I got this feeling from my father.

"When I admitted that, I realized I didn't trust my wife. I didn't think her capable or responsible. I realized I saw my wife as a little dumb child. And she had to spend money behind my back.

"At that point, I gave her the responsibility. I felt a tremendous burden lifted from my shoulders. I kept an eye on her the first month, and the second. It seemed to be going okay. From that point on, we were both responsible. Her spending pattern improved. She used more restraint and judgment. It became her money as well as mine."

What was at issue here in an otherwise happy marriage? It was more than who should write out the checks, more than Lisa's reckless spending sprees. Their analysis of their money problems did articulate the tensions, and mark out the areas of dispute. But the real argument wasn't about money per se; it was about emotional issues: trust, power, autonomy, and macho tendencies.

Lisa's overspending was pure rebellion at having no financial autonomy. Charles held all the economic cards, feeling he was some benefactor. Lisa felt this tyranny and lashed out. Luckily for them both, they heeded good advice. Once Charles recognized his "insulting patriarchal role," he was flexible enough to change. In so doing, power was equalized in the relationship and mutual trust flourished.

In our society, men still usually earn more than women, too often for the same work. Unless men and women share in controlling those earnings, a variety of conflicts emerge. One of the significant findings in *American Couples* was that "Partners who feel they have equal control over how the money is spent have a more tranquil relationship."[4] In other words, equity is crucial in money matters and marriage even if parity isn't possible yet *vis à vis* incomes.

In most marriages, even today's two-career marriages, money equals power. If a husband uses his higher earning power in a "controlling way" and abuses that power, chances are his wife will fight back. A basic sociological law is that people who are in a subservient role tend to strike out at their "oppressor." Often their kick is aimed at the other's most vulnerable sexual area.

In one blatant case, a businessman's wife, who was in a therapy group of mine, revolted after a severe argument with her husband by taking off, both literally and emotionally. There were economic repercussions in all this. For two weeks she flew around the country and finally she went to Europe. Using their joint credit cards, she bought expensive clothes, stayed at the finest hotels, and indulged in several affairs with men she picked up along the way. She spent a small fortune.

After this financially disastrous emotional escapade, the balance of power shifted in the relationship. The couple reconciled and spent the next several years paying off the outrageous debts accumulated during this "show" of power. Although this wife's rebellion cost them dearly, it did bring to light her grievances with his power-wielding and changed their relationship in a positive way.

It's easy to blame a controlling husband or an impulsive-spending wife for money squabbles. The fault can indeed rest in their spending allowances or habits, but the responsibility and blame must be spread around. Oftentimes that means backward, toward the couple's upbringing. A person's money mentality comes from his family, from family history. Most of the time it is this history that accounts for incompatibility in money styles.

In marital counseling, I've often encountered husbands and wives who come from different socioeconomic backgrounds. Because of this difference in early socialization, they have been conditioned to behave toward money in opposite ways. The case of Robert and Beth depicts this situation. Robert was the son of a widow from a small community where the motto was "Wear it out or make it do." His mother had to support herself and several other children besides Robert. She drilled into her children the importance of putting money aside for the inevitable rainy day. Robert never found this emotional stance toward money a problem until he got married.

For his wife, he chose Beth, the daughter of an urban family whose cultural values veered toward more gracious living. Their philosophy regarding economics could be summed up in expressions like "Money is for spending" and "Spend it now—it is later than you think."

This couple did not understand each other's internalized attitudes toward money. Beth accused Robert of trying to control her in a straitjacketed marriage with no financial freedom or power. Robert became disillusioned with Beth because she seemed to want everything now instead of being able to put off material desires. In the back of his mind, that rainy day loomed; in the back of hers, Judgment Day pressed hard. She felt compelled to get in all the good times while the getting was good; he had to prepare for disaster. Contrary economic mentalities, family histories, and time frames took this couple to the edge of divorce.

Initially, in the heat of their fights over money, Robert and Beth feared they had an unsolvable dilemma, but fortunately conflict turned out to be manageable. In counseling, Robert and Beth learned that neither was trying to control or punish the other by exercising "silly notions" about money and spending. They came to an understanding of just how each had been emotionally conditioned to behave in a certain way financially. Once they intellectually digested their differences, emotionally they were able to control their reactions. They went from irrational fighting to a rational understanding, and devised ways to compromise her spending imperatives with his spending phobias.

Robert and Beth were both potential Contenteds in their money styles. Having sorted through their one obstacle to economic harmony—family history—they were able to resolve each other's difficulties and get to those contented feelings.

DIVORCE

When couples can't resolve their incompatibilities and areas of conflict, financial or otherwise, they turn to divorce. Till-death-do-us-part marriage vows oftentimes deteriorate into legal battles to the death, as depicted in the 1989 film "The War of the Roses." Money fights continue and often escalate. Now the couples are pitted against each other not to run one household, but to divvy up assets and create two.

Aside from these practical monetary decisions, money often plays a devious role in divorce proceedings. Money settlement conflicts become more of a vehicle for expression of hostility between spouses than anything else. Money becomes the weapon each hurls at the other.

A psychiatrist I interviewed was very candid in revealing some of the financial machinations that surrounded his own divorce. Herb, fifty-four, had a number of perceptive insights into the connection of money and his divorce. His psychiatric background, his male biases, and his goals all shed light on this classic matrimonial battleground.

Herb told me, "She asked for a phenomenal amount of money. She asked for more alimony than I was making after taxes! She had the power of the law and I was not aware of my rights at the time. She was trying to take from me what money meant to me, which was freedom, freedom from having to work. She was going to force me to work for ten cents on the dollar.

"What galled me was she espoused a women's liberation position but when it came right down to it, she was out to get all she could from me! She just rationalized the whole thing. When we first split, she was spending a thousand dollars a week, on I don't know what. I analyzed it as a complete act of hitting me where it hurt most—in the pocketbook.

"When we first married fifteen years ago, she claimed to have a lot of bad feelings about money. She spouted how women shouldn't live off men, that they should earn their own money. But she never went out and did it. I felt I was making money for both of us. I offered to give her a bank account and set her up in a business. As a matter of fact, she had such an emotional thing about taking my money that I set up a phony system.

"I would keep $500 cash in the house in a certain place. She would quietly go and take money so it wouldn't be like she was taking it from me. It was a dumb game we played. When the money was gone, I'd replenish it. It gave me a good feeling because part of my heritage was that a man who supports his family is a man. I resented her inability to openly acknowledge that I made money and did that.

"I don't feel my wife, Marilyn, helped me make money. She opposed most everything I did. She never backed any of my actions. She was against my investments which paid off. She always talked about not having any money because there was very little in our bank account. We were 'poor' because I would borrow to invest in a building. Then years ago I made $50,000 on a piece of land and gave her $10,000.

"I don't want to destroy her financially in this divorce. I'd like to give her what I think she needs, enough for her and the two kids to live reasonably and comfortably, not to have to worry. What we are doing is classic. I've had patients do it in my practice: We are using money as a battleground.

"She's being unreasonable and I feel resentful. She doesn't need or deserve half my property as far as I'm concerned. I don't want to give it to her. I earned all that money. Her unreasonable demands crumble my plan to not work so hard past the age of fifty. Originally I had a master plan. She's no longer part of my life, except as a drain and a liability. It's less than charity because at least when you give money to charity, people are nice and say thank you. All I get from her no matter what I give is hostility. And I really resent her women's-lib hypocrisy. If she had any principles, she wouldn't act this way!"

Herb sees things only from his own point of view. Is the money all his? Are accumulated holdings in the course of a marriage a husband's personal bankroll to which a wife has no claim? Should a wife be "grateful" for alimony, or entitled to half of all assets for her role in their union? These questions provide the crux of disagreements during divorce. Money provides the fuel for battles which are highly emotional and mutually destructive. Herb may not be right in his male assessment of the facts, but he is right on target about how money fights are a classic rite of divorce proceedings.

It's clear money fights are part and parcel of most marriages and can persist even when those marriages themselves fail. What's a couple to do to diffuse their financial conflicts before these conflicts diffuse their love for one another?

Negotiating the romantic deal—marriage—means coordinating diverse money styles, family histories, and economic mentalities. The challenge of every marriage is for both spouses to learn to decipher each other's money style and to strike a compromise.

The arguments in the money battle change as society changes. During the 1970s the agenda was often women's fiscal dependence versus autonomy and choice. Homemakers wanted to be credited for their contributions and empowered financially. During the 1980s the agenda changed drastically as women went to work outside the home and families divided and regrouped as step-families. Financial issues are different now. Men and women each have their own money and "Whose money is it anyway?" has become a troubling question. Should her money pay bills or only his? Whose money should pay for children from a previous marriage, hers or his? Whose career is more valuable? If one spouse wants to move to pursue a job change, should the other's career receive equal weight in the decision, even if it pays less? These are all complicated questions that have to be negotiated in the context of running households, running marriages, and running lives.

Couples must face larger sociological questions along with day-to-day differences in spending patterns, priorities, and viewpoints regarding money. They must redefine money, and their masculinity and femininity as well. It's ironic that although so much has changed within the American marriage and family, certain attitudes remain the same. Recent research reveals that most couples still feel that the man should "provide for" the wife. Around 75 percent of couples still believed in the late 80s that it is important for husbands to provide financial security for wives and families. The man is still seen as the breadwinner, and yet fiscal relationships have taken on a number of new complications.

Money has always been and will always be an incendiary item on the marital agenda. My research leads me to conclude that focusing on money styles, their origins and their impact within a marriage, is a good way for a couple to get a handle on economic disputes. Once a couple learns the secrets of each other's money style—their overt differences and hidden, covert areas of conflict—they can effectively strike a balance between even the most incompatible features of their money personalities. A little fiscal knowledge is not a dangerous thing here, it's an important factor in a successful marriage.

5

Parents and "Learning the Value of a Dollar"

$\mathcal{E}$VERY PARENT affects his or her child's attitudes about money. The curriculum is both conscious and unconscious. The lesson is most often called "learning the value of a dollar."

The emphasis a parent places on money, the conflicts parents themselves have about money, the financial status of the child's family, and the specific approach a child's parents use in doling out money, all affect the development of a person's money style.

In response to the survey question, "How much emphasis did your parents place on your being financially successful?" and "Have you fulfilled their expectations?" 80 percent of the sample felt that their parents had placed considerable emphasis on earning money. Perhaps this figure would vary considerably in a socialist country where government is designed to meet more needs, and less emphasis is placed on financial success.

Financially speaking, 75 percent of the respondents felt they had fulfilled their parents' expectations. I also found that a direct correlation existed between people's earning power and the amount of emphasis placed on financial success by parents. The greater the financial push made by parents, the higher the income reached by the children as adults.

In the $20,000 to $30,000 income bracket, I found fewer than expected people whose parents had placed a great emphasis on money. While one would assume they'd push harder, as it turned out lower-income families did not place as much emphasis on earning money as higher income parents.

In the $100,000-plus income bracket, I found significantly more than expected people whose parents had placed great emphasis on earning money, and, conversely, fewer than expected whose parents apparently didn't take their status for granted, but programmed high aspirations into their children.

An emerging trend was clear: The higher the family income, the greater the stress on earning power, and the greater the likelihood of the child earning more. In other words, if parents hold up high financial standards for their children, the children are likely to aspire to and meet those fiscal goals. The financially successful and unsuccessful respondents were no more or less than a reflection of their parents' teachings and goals.

For a parent to realize he or she holds the earning power potential and financial future of their children in hand is a weighty thought and a huge responsibility. Parenting is central in money matters: both in where you end up financially and how you end up emotionally.

In the first part of this chapter, I will examine how some of the survey respondents learned their lessons on the value of the dollar in their socialization process. In the latter half, I suggest how parents can improve their lesson plan for the teaching of dollar values.

THE FAMILY MONEY TREE

An examination of how your parents influenced you in money

matters is a valuable exercise. It will suggest nuggets of insight into the origins of your money style and your emotional attitudes about money.

The following example of Steven, a very successful and very wealthy businessman, illustrates this point. Steven was trying to fathom how he had acquired his insatiable drive for money. He claimed his mother and father were hardly instrumental, being strictly middle class and not particularly inclined to teach him excessive ambition. Steven's commentary is revealing.

"My parents never did anything special about money. As a matter of fact, they paid very little attention to me in any way. I always felt that in my family I didn't exist."

After that confidential confession, I probed his early recollections a bit further. Suddenly, he blurted out, "Wait a minute, I just thought of something—my uncle. My mother constantly talked about my rich uncle! I'll tell you what seems right to me. I, to this day, have desperately sought my mother's love. I feel I never got it. Maybe when I was a kid I set out to become the rich male uncle she idolized. He was in business like I am. I thought if I got rich, like him, she'd approve and love me. I think that's what motivated me. But it hasn't worked."

It depends upon how you look at Steven's success. Perhaps he didn't succeed in getting his mother's approval or love, but he did become a very wealthy businessman. Steven's insight about his mother and his affluent uncle provided some answers to his questions about his money style, and, perhaps, some freedom from his childhood wounds.

My research clearly revealed that money, love, and parental approval are often entwined. I've found family dramas to be laden with monetary themes in my psychodramatic therapy work. The following session with Bill reveals this issue. Bill, a thirty-five-year-old lawyer, was filled with rage toward his father. Initially, he told me, "No matter how much money I make, I still don't get my father's approval. In the last five years, my yearly earnings doubled. When I tell him this, he'll say something like, 'That's nice, but Joe or Jim or some cousin of mine is doing better.' He really gets me mad."

Bill went on to explain that his father had been critical of him all his life. Rather than praising his son, he always held back pride and held out another *carrot*—the example of someone who did better. Bill worked harder, constantly trying to win that approval. Earning more money became the medium of the sought-after message of love and approval.

Bill tried to resolve his conflicts about his father in a psychodrama session. In one role-playing scene, an auxiliary actor took the role of Bill's dad, this time giving complete approval with the line, "You're a fine lawyer and you are earning a fantastic amount of money!" Bill responded with a beaming face, tears filling his eyes as the two ended the scene with a hug.

As is usual in psychodrama technique, a discussion followed. Bill realized he equated love with approval, but limited solely to the issue of money, earning power. Surely his father's love could be measured in ways other than his reaction to a pay check! Bill's continuing need to earn more money so he would eventually please his dad created his Insatiable money style.

What surfaced in Bill's psychodrama was that his father's behavior was a double-edged sword. On the one hand, not getting the pat on the back for a job well paid and well done was indeed emotionally painful. But on the other hand, Bill's father had purposely or inadvertently given him motivation to push forward professionally. Bill's final challenge was to let go of his adolescent need for paternal approval but not to let go of his drive to succeed financially in a more rational, less insatiable way.

Robert, a well-known Hollywood screenwriter, found his family attitudes about money filled with complex answers, explanations, and warnings. His money mentality was formed early.

He recalled, "Growing up, we were poor but honest people. My mother had to work to supplement my father's meager income. My mother was always good for throwaway lines which I later incorporated into my novels, lines like 'I love you, Bob, but I can't tell you.' She was incapable of giving affection openly. I see now, looking back, how clever she was, pitting me and my two brothers [against each other] in a competition to get her approval. Getting it simply meant earning money and giving it to her. As kids, she had all three of us boys doing odd jobs—paper delivery, working in a store, things like that. The one who brought in the most money was the star of the week."

Money was the paramount lesson Robert learned. Repeating that lesson, rebelling against it, became the barometer of his professional output and creative satisfaction.

He continued, "I've done a few screenplays. In Hollywood wheeling and dealing, there is an expression, the bottom line, meaning how much [money]. When I began to get some credits and win awards, I'd call my mother to tell her. All she ever wanted to know was, what's the bottom line. Thinking back, she never cared about the work, just how much was the payoff.

"I would often do projects for very little money or no money if I thought they had artistic merit. I was rebelling against my mother, I see now.

"My mother never had a good word to say about any of my work, despite press attention or TV exposure. Recently, I wrote a book and sent her a copy as usual. A week later she called. She went on and on with kudos. I was waiting for the bottom-line shoe to drop, or some negative zinger, but none did—it was all approval. I hung up the telephone, stunned. My wife looked at me and asked, 'Who was that?' Looking faint, I mumbled that Mom liked the book. It was the first time in my life I got a positive response with no money questions. She had always said before, 'What you do doesn't count, only money counts.' "

Robert's mother's obsessive money mentality perverted his creative judgments. He came to judge his work not on its quality, but on its price tag, but his judgments were the reverse of his mother's. He "hated" his commercial successes, often giving value only to more obscure, less commercial projects. While rebelling, he sometimes wrote his most creative work. In therapy, he learned how to develop his own judgment of his work, apart from his mother. This didn't slowdown his productivity, and he achieved greater self-satisfaction from his work without all of his past concerns about money being the bottom line.

In Laura's case her parents had created in her a fear of poverty, even though as an adult she was married to a relatively affluent man. "I came from a very poor background, and I'm deadly afraid of being poor again. My husband had to force me to buy anything! Money in the bank is my security blanket."

While Laura and her husband realized she had a near-phobia about spending and hoarding money, they disagreed for a long time on the solution. Laura liked to just flippantly toss off criticism, claiming most marriages are between one spender and one saver. However, once she witnessed her anxieties repeating themselves in her own daughter's activities, she changed her mind.

She said, "I noticed when I took my little girl to buy clothes, she was very careful. She'd check all the price tags, and she was very reluctant to buy anything. That's not what I wanted for her. I want her to have everything I never had. But she resisted spending money, and I have to assume she picked this up from me."

If there is one positive upshot of this version of the "sins of the mother" being visited upon the child, it is that Laura finally acknowledged her own financial phobia and worked it out in therapy.

In commenting on parent and child issues related to money, *New York Times* "Parent and Child" columnist Lawrence Kutner stated: "Understanding money is one of the most confusing, difficult and emotion-laden tasks children face. For many, it was a subject seldom discussed. Money was as mysterious as sex, as steeped in ritual as religion and as volatile as politics."[1]

In view of those truths, I interviewed children about their financial education. As they say, from out of the mouths of babes came some money talk well worth listening to.

Gary, age ten:

Gary is from a single-parent family, living in the upper middle class suburb of Chatsworth, California. According to Gary, "If you gave me $1000 I would buy a bunch of new baseball bats, some baseballs, a glove, and some new spikes. I would be happy with $1000, because that's a lot of money. I don't know why I feel better when I have money, but I know I just do. My mom doesn't do too much about teaching me about money, because she doesn't know what to do with money herself. I always tell her that she shouldn't tell me what to do with my money because she can't even pay all the bills herself. I would never work without making a lot of money, unless I was a major league baseball player. I would play for the Dodgers for free, but I know big league baseball players earn a lot of money anyway."

Ricky, age twelve:

The child of a wealthy Beverly Hills family, Ricky declared, "My parents haven't taught me a lot about money. I know what it is, and I can see what it buys them. That's about what I know about money. It feels good when I have money to buy the things I want.

"The worst thing about money is having to ask my old man for it all the time. He gives me these dumb lectures about the value of money and how hard he worked to get it. Listening to him is really a pain in the ass. He gives me what I want anyway. Why does he have to make me pay for it by listening to his dumb stories?"

Ricky's dad seems to deserve an E for effort. At least he's trying to get a financial message across. Lisa's father, a supermarket checker, is also trying to lay some fiscal foundation, but according to Lisa, he's missing the mark.

Lisa, age sixteen:

"My father has tried to teach me about money, but he's not a very good example. He once went broke and my mom still reminds him about it every time she gets mad at him. Money is very important because without money you can't do anything. You end up being a slave to your parents. Plus, you always want to look your best. I do feel I have to keep up with my friends. I have to keep up with them, there's no doubt about that. I like to go out with guys who have money and dress nice and have a cool car. It makes me feel good to be with a guy like that. When my friends see me, I know they're jealous. Lots of times, though, I have to settle for guys with less bread. When I get older, though, I'll make sure I fall in love with a rich guy. Who wants to struggle like my mom does?"

Lisa claims her parents aren't good examples, but she has learned a great deal even if some if it should be unlearned.

Don, age sixteen:

Don is middle class, spending his summer vacation working a construction job, hating every minute under the blazing sun, but doing it for the money. He said: "Money is the only reason I work. My parents have raised me to understand money. Money can definitely buy you power and freedom. Power is the most important because with it we don't have to be nobodies. Everybody wants some power. There are many different ways to be powerful, but the easiest way is money. When you have money you can pick your friends. I've seen plenty of movies and TV shows where wheeler-dealers make a fast buck and have plenty of women, drive a Rolls, and live in a big house. If I ever get a chance I'd go for it. One more thing—rich girls. Not only do rich girls have more money, they have superior manners, they don't have as many hang-ups, they always look their best, and they know how to treat a guy the right way." (Don didn't explain what he meant by "the right way.")

Whether they recognize the learning process or not, all of these children are learning money attitudes from their parents. Don is clear about money and power lessons, and certain that rich people are better. Lisa has learned well the lesson of keeping up with the Joneses—adolescent-style. She also seems to agree with Don's preference for rich suitors. Ricky's learning about money means manipulation, especially as he sees himself the captive audience for his dad's dumb stories. And Gary is certain that money makes him feel better, even though intellectually he doesn't grasp the money/self-esteem connection.

An understanding of the process of passing down fiscal values is in order if we are to learn from some of their mistakes. I have created a lesson plan of do's and don'ts to help parents recognize and eliminate inappropriate economic strategies and replace them with sound financial policies.

MONEY DON'TS FOR PARENTS

• *Don't buy your way out of guilt feelings*

In an era of working mothers, two-career marriages, latch-key children, and day care, guilt is a national epidemic among parents, especially working moms. Often mothers try to do what overworked fathers tried to do before them: Pay their guilt off with a few bucks.

Sarah, ten years old, said, "If my mother doesn't get home for dinner on time or when I've got sitters a lot during the week, she gives me an extra dollar or two on Saturday."

Jason, eleven, said, "Whenever my dad comes home from a business trip he says, 'Here's something to bolster your allowance,' as if that's supposed to make up for the two weeks he wasn't at home."

Paying off guilt doesn't work. It's too transparent. Guilt is one of those problems that only gets worse if you throw money at it.

To a baby or young child, time and love carry no price tags. If and when we adults try to substitute dollars and cents for love and attention, we teach a peculiar hook-up of love, money, time, and guilt. In such a misspent transaction, we devalue ourselves in our children's eyes because they do see through us and we devalue them by trying to bribe them to forgive us for our own "failings."

Apologies for absence or ill temper should never be made with our wallets either. Some parents try to ransom an impatient outburst or an irrational foul mood with dollars.

According to nine-year-old Paula, "When my mom is real mean to me over nothing, she sometimes gives me a dollar afterwards and tells me to buy myself something. Nothing's changed, she was still mean to me, except she thinks the dollar evens things out."

This well-meaning parent, who might have had a bad day, apparently felt that giving would accomplish more than just saying "I'm sorry." In this case, the act of giving became only a cheap shot. A more effective gesture would have been that apology with an explanation of the reasons behind her lapse of patience.

Children are naturally shrewd in emotional matters. As Ben, age eight, indignantly told me, "If my dad wants some peace and quiet, he should just say so. I'll leave him alone. It's stupid of him to send me to the movies just to get rid of me."

Parental guilt is probably unavoidable, given the pace and responsibilities of the times. Parents are entitled to want time away from their kids. Parents are only human; moments of irrational, ill-tempered explosions are inevitable. But settling guilty scores should not be a financial matter.

- ### *Don't put a higher price on things than you put on people*

Karen is an angry young seventeen-year-old. Some of her anger is justifiably aimed at her parents, "My parents have placed their entire emphasis on getting wealthy. That's all they ever wanted to do since they were young. Now they've done it. Did it make them happy? No— oh for a few minutes or months, but as they push fifty they are beginning to notice that they missed a few things, sentimental, romantic things that they had no time to stop for on their way up.

"My dad's made a fortune in television. He's a brilliant man, but he never had the time to give me any of his brilliance because he was too busy making money. He has spent his life acquiring money. My mother has spent her life spending it. She's out there every day on Rodeo Drive. My psychiatrist says when she spends she feels good, younger than her fifty years for a few hours, and she gets even with my father, who usually seduces any woman he can. Life in Bel Air isn't all it's cracked up to be! My parents gave us plenty of money, things, psychiatry, but no love."

Don't let your value system upgrade material things at the expense of people, family, parenting, and marriage.

This mistake can be made in a profound way on the large scale or in little everyday mistakes. For instance, if a child breaks an ashtray we may blurt out, "You stupid kid. That cost me ten dollars." We should really say, "I'm angry because you didn't respect what's mine." Unless we separate the child's act from the child, he may think he is less important than a ten dollar item. Or that breaking something cheap is okay as opposed to breaking something expensive. Or that things are more costly than a parent's love.

It's hard for parents not to mesh issues of love and money, which brings us to the next don't.

- ### *Don't punish financially (even if you reward financially)*

As one young man told me, "The theory of allowances is the very core and foundation of the U.S. kid's economic system." Allowances can be used or misused.

In middle-income groups I found parents tended to conceal money difficulties from children, use money to show love and approval, and withhold it to mete out punishment. Many parents consider the allowance the tool that hammers home morality. For instance, the child gets five dollars a week unless . . . unless he doesn't empty the dishwasher, mow the lawn, or complete whatever chores are involved in the allowance deal; unless he is disrespectful to elders; and so on. Sometimes this morality-for-money backfires, reaping immorality, dishonesty.

One twelve-year-old's confession went like this. "If I only tell them the good stuff that's happening in school, I get my allowance. If I tell them everything, I don't. So I just talk about the stuff they want to hear and not the rest."

And another: "I start cleaning up my room and being nice to my parents by about Wednesday evening. That way I'll be sure to get my allowance money on Friday night."

If an allowance becomes a means of coercion, a money-is-power lesson comes on too strongly. Jim complained frustratedly: "If I haven't done well in school my father won't give me my money. Once all my friends were going to see *Batman I,* and I got a bad report from school. He wouldn't give me my money so I couldn't go. I cried, started throwing things, and really blew up. I felt like punching him. I felt like running away. I can't wait till I get older and earn my own money."

While it is legitimate to tie an allowance in with chores or even study habits, it is not fair to make an allowance a catch-all to teach every moral lesson in the book for children. The only lesson a child may learn in such an inconsistent set-up is a Machiavellian one.

MONEY DO'S FOR PARENTS

• *Do teach work steps*

It is important for children to learn where money comes from, how parents obtain it. The connection of work and money is at the root of allowances. It can also be taught in other ways. For example, taking your child to your place of business is extremely effective. Don't forget, young children see money as just being there. A parent has to teach them how much is there and where it comes from.

If a child is brought up to believe money comes his way just for breathing, trouble is in the wind. This lesson is especially important in affluent families, those that worked their way up and those that were born at the top of the fiscal ladder. Listen to one dad's mistake.

"I was a poor kid myself and any money I got I had to scrounge for or work for. I guess I didn't want that for my son. Now I can afford to give him most things he wants. I love my son and I'll admit it, I've indulged his every whim. I've been lazy. If he wants to go to Disneyland or eat out with friends, good old dad gives him some cash.

"I never gave him an allowance because I knew he'd blow it fast and then I couldn't refuse him when he came around later in the week for more money. Part of my problem is laziness. I don't want to fight with him, so I pretty much give him what he wants. And the other thing is, sometimes he's just a pain and money gets him out of the house, playing pinball or going to a movie, and off my back."

While this dad's doling-out style has assorted motives, some good and some admittedly not, he is endangering his son's financial future. By not teaching the work steps, he's crippling his fourteen-year-old son's motivation and his understanding of how money is earned in the real world. By fiscally "spoiling" a child, you are rearing a person who will feel entitled to get money at whim, who will harbor the attitude the world owes him a living. Unless a parent plans on doling out money for the rest of the child's life, he had better nip the practice in the proverbial bud.

• Do teach an economic agenda

The value of work other than financial reward, the principle of discretionary income, and the lesson of delayed gratification.

When should a child go out and get a job? No other question has raised such controversy. According to Dr. Roy Grinker, Jr. of the Institute of Psychosomatic and Psychiatric Research at Chicago's Michael Reese Medical Center, early work history was the common denominator in a study of mentally healthy young males. The healthy child cannot stand being idle. Children from age three to eight will usually work hard without any thought of reward. They identify themselves with adults and their work is like a fantasy. For the nine to twenty age group, reality sets in. Dull manual labor is very burdensome. However, they will work endlessly on old cars, radios, bicycles, and similar projects that interest them. Laziness in children is the exception, caused by poor health or lack of interests.[2]

The implication of Dr. Grinker's research is that work is naturally valuable and interesting to healthy young people. The decision parents must face is when to encourage or allow "paid" work. Studies have recently shown that rather than teaching the positive value of work, paid work for teens tends to teach the opposite. In a ten-year survey of teens at the Institute for Social Research, University of Michigan, social psychologists Jerald Bachman, Lloyd Johnson, and Patrick O'Malley found that young people's ideas about work are shaped by the jobs they experience as teens. That turned out to be bad news. Three-quarters of high school seniors hold part-time jobs, averaging sixteen to twenty hours a week, and often netting more than $200 per month. Unfortunately, most seniors reported their jobs make little or no use of their skills or abilities. Many characterized these jobs as the "kind people do just to earn money."[3] In other words, teens are coming away with the concept of work as unrewarding, monotonous, just a necessary evil to make money—not for the lesson we would have them learn, that work can be self-satisfying and intrinsically valuable.

This finding and others have raised serious questions about whether or not we should push teens into fast-food restaurants, gas stations, and department stores, where they are not learning appropriate dollar-value lessons. Parents have a responsibility to teach their young that work can be satisfying in a variety of ways other than just financial.

The handling of discretionary income is another bone of contention in the should-teens-work controversy. Somehow, parents have to drive home the lesson that most earnings should pay for necessities, and only limited resources should go for "play" expenses. In Bachman's survey, more than 60 percent of the teens reported that their money went for eating out, clothing, and entertainment. Fewer than 10 percent contributed at least half their paycheck toward family living expenses.

While these figures attest to rising affluence within families, they don't attest to good long-range economic values and management. Teenagers who learn money is for care-free hedonistic pleasure are going to have a difficult time budgeting for life's expenses and adjusting to the normal sacrifices most adults must make in money matters.

Chances are, they may never learn the crucial lesson of delayed gratification. Spending it now, or saving it for a later day is an important choice. This young man's decision, to go or not go to college, is one example. "My dad wants me to go to college, but I don't think I'll be able to cut that. As soon as I graduate high school I'm going to work so I can make money and buy some of the things I want so bad, like clothes and especially a car."

Immediate gratification or delayed gratification regarding money is important; and it's a lesson that must be taught before a child is college age. Even toddlers can learn about choices—for example, one piece of candy now or several later after supper, is a choice involving the principle of gratification.

Parents need an economic agenda in order to impart worthwhile fiscal values. Some experts suggest children be included in, instead of excluded from, family money accounting and planning sessions. Holding family powwows to discuss major purchases, or bringing home a week's salary in cash and piling it into categories like mortgage or rent, utilities, food, insurance, et cetera, may teach real lessons about discretionary income, how buying one item entails doing without others, and the value of saving for a rainy day.

- **Do allow mistakes to be made at home for the lesson of financial independence**

Money management can be taught by example, by holding out a good role model, but also by holding back. Children need leeway and freedom as well as guidance and rules, as the following story illustrates.

A sixteen-year-old boy went without snacks and movies and saved up three weeks' allowance for a football. He said, "My father was furious. He wanted me to buy something important, but that football *was* important to me."

By questioning the child's choice of purchase, the parent negated the lesson of financial independence his son had apparently mastered. Saving is one lesson, spending is another, and financial independence yet another. Parents need to give their children room to grow even if it sometimes looks as if they are going to hang themselves in the process.

If a child mows lawns all day for fifty dollars and blows it in half an hour's worth of jet-skiing for himself and a friend, let him draw his own conclusions from that expensive date. Making mistakes is part of all learning, including financial lessons.

- **Do separate dollar values from other values, and emphasize nonmaterialistic values as well**

A study article about the values of today's college freshmen, titled "The One Who Has the Most Toys When He Dies Wins," seems to reveal that today's students are more materialistic than ever. That title was conceived to be a bumper sticker summing up predominant values based on a sample of 300,000 of the nation's college freshmen. Pollsters Alexander Astin and Kenneth C. Green of the Cooperative Institutional Research Program, an affiliate of the University of California, Los Angeles, quizzed students every fall from 1966 to 1986. The study revealed that about 70 percent of college freshmen said that a major reason for attending college was "to be able to make more money," and a like number said, "to be very well off financially" was an essential or very important goal. These figures were up one third in ten years. Freshmen planning to major in business have nearly doubled over the last two decades, from 14 percent to 27 percent.[4]

In the 1960s, few students majored in business, many more were involved with developing a career in social service. It was inconceivable back then that business leaders like Donald Trump and Lee Iaccoca would become the cult heroes they are today. The times have changed, but at what expense?

In the course of my research, one young man told me, "My father keeps telling me I have expensive tastes. I like skiing and surfing, and all that. And he tells me that if I don't do better in school, I'll never get a good job or earn decent money. He says the only way I'll ever earn any big money is to go to college."

The boy's father's advice is, of course, accurate in one sense. In his focus on money, though, he's left out the joys and advantages of knowledge for knowledge's sake, how learning and higher education are existentially useful in life beyond money.

This parent, and—judging from surveys like Astin and Green's—many others need to highlight values other than money, including values such as educational achievement, helping others, and self-esteem. Astin and Green noted that twenty years ago 80 percent of freshmen cited "developing meaningful philosophy of life" as an important or essential goal. Today's statistic dropped to about 41 percent. The pollsters suggest that, to today's young, making money precludes the need for a philosophy of life; or worse, making money may be seen as the philosophy of life in itself.[5]

If money is programmed to loom so large in our children's minds, by the year 2100 the Insatiable money style may dominate our society. Nonmaterialistic values are needed to balance out their world if they are to find contentment. In an era when rock stars and athletes are selling themselves to the highest bidder for any product from sodas to sneakers, and doctors are often investment bankers, public servants are scandalous scoundrels, and business people corporate raiders, it is important that parents address more substantial issues beyond the dollar sign.

Part II
Money Talks

6

The Rich Are *Different*

"The rich are different," began F. Scott Fitzgerald.
"Yes, they have more money," Hemingway
chimed in, finishing off the sentence.

*W*EALTHY PEOPLE are different, set apart not only in terms of where they live but by their freedom to travel. Wealth is a great divider in our society. Part of our American ethos implies that money produces a sense of well-being, of happiness. So the great majority of people are socialized to go after material success as an emotional balm, to soothe and smooth out all problems.

If money did indeed deliver happiness, and happiness was having money, then it would logically follow that the rich are not only different but across the board, happy. Of course we know that this is not the case.

Our voyeuristic obsession with the rich and the lifestyles of the rich and famous reached a cultural apogee in the 80s. Vast audiences seemed to enjoy "rich" soap operas like *Dallas, Dynasty,* and other television programs whose central theme was rich people and their problems. A plethora of celebrity biographies took the publishing industry by storm and retold the same story of emotionally poor and unhappy little rich boys and girls. The appeal of such affluent hard-luck tales lies in a thinly disguised yet prevalent hostility most people have toward the superrich. Many people outside of wealthy borders want to see the rich suffer with their problems. Most people don't want to hear the rich live on a bed of roses.

Do they or don't they? What do wealthy people say about their lives? Are they happy? Do they have different dilemmas than ordinary people? Or do they lead ordinary lives but in a different tax bracket?

I interviewed a variety of wealthy people for this study. Some of what they said about money will be what you'd expect, but hardly all. Being rich does have advantages, but it also has its own set of difficulties. Being rich in the 80s, though, has broken new ground for the leisured class. In an ironic turn, the 1980s have given birth to more millionaires with less leisurely lifestyles.

The interview I carried out with Margo Lederer, daughter of a millionaire businessman and the famous advice columnist Ann Landers, serves as a good introduction to the rich. Ms. Lederer touched on a number of issues which provide valuable insights into the lives of the wealthy in America. Her story illuminates many sides of the coin, because she went from poor to rich in her own youth, and gives us a perspective on her upbringing and the upbringing of her children as well.

She comments insightfully on the pitfalls and challenges of living rich, "We were not always wealthy. Up until the time I was seven, there really was no money in our family. I remember in California before I was seven—I slept on a cot in the kitchen. We lived in a lot of towns, not living well. We lived here in Chicago once before we moved here when I was older. I had the bedroom and my parents slept in a Murphy bed in the living room. So I remember a really modest kind of living. Not poor, but nothing going on. All of a sudden there was money. My father and mother both began to earn a lot of money—after a long period of financial struggle.

"My mother had a psychologist friend who told her that I should be allowed to have anything I wanted so I would understand that we were rich. The order he gave to my mother was 'This girl has been poor, and now you must dramatically prove to her she's rich.' It was clearly communicated to me.

"At first my parents just socked the money away. They didn't start to spend it really until I was fourteen, and then it started. We lived in a very fine building. I had my own telephone at an early age, and I had charge accounts at all the good stores. I particularly remember going to Saks at the age of fourteen, buying a Bermuda short outfit, a cashmere sweater in cornflower blue—it then cost a hundred and fifty dollars. And there was never any hassle about it. My mother thought all that was fine. And I remember my father, when I was in college, used to send cases of things to me at school. For example, as a child I loved Bosco. When I went to camp, they would send Bosco. But other kids would get maybe a can of Bosco, I would get a case.

"I had my own charge card to Lochobers—it was a restaurant in Boston, where I was a student at Brandeis University. It was really marvelous, and I mentioned to Father that I really liked it. Well, comes another charge card with a note, 'Feel free to take your friends.' I also used to go to New York often for the weekends when I was in college and I would always have a limousine meet me. I would tell Father when I was going and I was always cared for at the St. Regis as though I were a little girl, but in fact I was eighteen, nineteen. . . . I was handed chunks of money to go out and spend.

"I didn't think much about it until later on when I was analyzed as a married woman in my mid-twenties. Money had such peculiar meanings to me. It was almost a kind of 'I like you,' or 'If you're worth something as a person I'll give you a lot of money.' That's the way I've always felt about money.

"I was identified at Brandeis as a rich girl, but there were a lot of rich kids there. Charles Revson's son was there. The child of Revlon's executive vice-president was there. A kid named Bob Renfield was there, whose family owns Gilbey's Gin and Haig Scotch. I was not the only rich one, and I was not the richest."

[Did you find any friends, male or female, whom you felt were trying to be friends with you because you had money?]

"You know, that's interesting. I've always had my antenna up on that because of my famous mother and my rich father. To my knowledge that has never happened. While I used it and I liked being a rich kid, I was very careful about what that had to do with friendship. I think I made it. Of course, you never really know, do you?"

[There must have been some male pursuers or beaus that you suspected may have gone after you for your money?]

"If they did, it never got very far; but I have no recollection of some guy trying to get into my father's business or anything like that. But, maybe there were a few.

"My peak experience with money is rather peculiar. My first marriage was to a man who became very rich and who was poor when I married him. When that marriage started to become rather empty for me and unpleasant and hurtful, I decided to get him. We were separated and about to get divorced. I went to Saks—in Chicago—and I went into the designer dress department and I bought $4800 worth of dresses, and charged it. To this day I get handwritten notes—I haven't been back, but that sales department writes me handwritten notes, 'Please come, we're having a showing. Please come.'

"It was like a harpoon I used on my ex-husband. And when he got the bill it really hit home how angry I was.

"I never received a lot of money from my family until I was twenty-one and until I was married. As a kid, although I could buy what I wanted and got many things, I was always told by my parents, who were then both rich—my mother had been left money, my mother had earned money, my father had made a lot of money, so there was all kinds of money—I was told that I was not being left anything because they didn't believe in inheritances. They were leaving it to charity. Well, I believed it and I was mad as hell for many years about that. I thought this was really lousy. I knew kids with trust funds, but if that's their belief, it's okay, because it's their money. I was mad at them, but I understood from whence this came.

"They were really kidding about not leaving me money. They had said they never wanted me to carry on as an heiress because I might attract the wrong kind of fellow. I wasn't told until recently that they were kidding. My feeling when I was told was a sense of relief—Oh, good, it's mine. I always thought it should properly be mine anyway. At that point it was such a positive thing, better that way than if I had been told as a youngster there's a five million dollar trust fund. When I was twenty-nine they said, 'We were just kidding. It's not going to charity, it's all yours.'

"Do I think my first husband married me for my money? Well, I wouldn't put it that way. I have come to believe that people get interested in a lot of things. I think my family interested him in terms of their being well connected, my mother on a national, sort of important level, and my father on a business level. And my father was of value to him. This guy would have made it if my father had not introduced him around and if my father had not guaranteed notes at the bank, but he would have made it a few years later than he did. My father did help him and was very useful to him in his business career.

"It's strange, we played a game he developed, a fantasy that I was a waitress whom he had rescued from the corner greasy spoon. It got so muddled in his mind that we were of any use to him, that it was like a joke.

"We never argued about money. I could do whatever I wanted. You see, he was so guilty on so many levels that the least he had to offer me was total financial freedom. You see, he was an alcoholic. When you drink, you behave poorly on a number of levels. He was constantly letting me down and disappointing me and hurting me. So if it quieted me, even temporarily, to go spend, that was fine. Also, I was going to say it's a Jewish husband's thing, but it isn't. What a wife has or wears or buys is some reflection of how well the guy is doing. So it's a very simple statement. If the wife is bedecked in diamonds, then the man is doing okay. If there are many mink coats, people just know that you're making it. I was a showcase for him. So he never interfered with my spending. We had expensive cars. I never did the car picking myself, but I had a Rolls-Royce, a Mercedes, and a Jaguar. I had every fine car there is, usually foreign. I had a Cadillac, I guess, and a Lincoln. The Rolls was given to me by my husband. He always wanted one, but he was ashamed to drive it. I was quite young and felt it looked a little too much. We mainly used the Cadillac."

[Being rich, how do you feel when you see people who are poor? Do you feel guilty?]

"No. I guess because I've always tried to help poor people. I really am quite charitable. I would help people either quietly, or through organizations, and I never connected it to me. I don't think I ever had guilt. It never occurred to me, how come I have it and they don't. Of course, I didn't see a lot of that stuff. Somebody once drove me through a section in Chicago and they said, 'Here's where the poor Jews live.' And I didn't know there were any poor Jews. That's ethnic craziness, to think that they're all rich.

"There are black poor people you knew, of course. But not poor Jews. That never occurred to me.

"I have very little understanding of money. I don't know how hard it is to make a lot of money. I really take it for granted. Money has always been something there to take care of me. And I never had to go after it.

"I've earned my own money, too, but it never felt as wonderful as people said it felt. Women carry on. They've lived with a husband twenty years, they finally go to work, they say, 'This two hundred dollars a week from the dress shop is such a terrific thing.' I never got that feeling. And I was making a lot more than that when I finally did go to work. It never felt just wonderful. I mean, money is money. You put it in the account and you do something with it.

"When I split up with my husband, we did get into a funny thing about money. He wanted to stay married and he tried to hold me with money. He really thought that I would not divorce him if he kept asking for things in the settlement. So he asked for all the paintings that he wanted. We did have some fine ones. We may have had a half a million dollars' worth of paintings. He thought that would really stop me, and I said, 'Here, take whatever you want.' And I really believed that that was correct. It was his taste that had picked those paintings and his money that had paid for them. And I always had a very clear sense this was his money. And I understood his emotional difficulty with the divorce. He wanted to stay married, I wanted to get away. So I didn't ask for anything for myself. I received no real settlement. I got very modest alimony till I remarried, but the children are beautifully taken care of by him.

"The children, to this day, literally cost me nothing. We were separated for two years. There was very lavish temporary support, I mean extraordinary. I received seven thou a month to take care of whatever would come up. And it was at that point that I went to work so that there was even more money.

"How do I manage money with my children? That's interesting. They are very rich children. They will have much more money than I ever will have when they get their inheritances. I'm talking about the end money that you're ever going to get. Very rich children, these. In the beginning I used to say to them, by design: 'No, we can't afford it.' It occurred to me once that's not true, I'm lying, they could have anything they want. A psychiatrist who specializes in children mentioned to me that rich kids know they're rich. They see where they're going. They see how the adults in their family live. They see the gifts. You can't fool them. So, on another level, now I'm having a discussion with their father and some money managers setting up stuff for the kids. What do you do about philosophy, do you tell little kids, 'One day you're going to have a lot of money,' so they'll be prepared and they'll grow up with it, or does that rob them of motivation? Or do you say nothing until they're twenty-one and you have to tell them?

"I haven't really decided how to handle it. I've talked to other kids like me who maybe have come into their money already. I mean, the parents don't have to die. The consensus seems to be you shouldn't articulate too heavily that there's going to be a lot of money. You don't really have to say anything about it, like 'You don't have to work, honey, because Grandpa's taken care of everything.' It's time enough when the kids are out of school to say, 'All right, in five years or ten years this is what is going to happen, and we want you to think about it.' But I really understand now there's no need to tell little kids about trust funds or a million dollars."

[What are your fears for them with regard to money? You have a reference point in your father. Your father became rich and famous and your mother did also, partially related to a motivation which had something to do with money. Do you concern yourself about it all? Why should your kids work or do anything?]

"That's a mixed-up issue for me. I really believe that people are achievers, whether it's by making a lot of money or a wonderful name, because they're very good at what they do—I think these people have a neurotic motivation. For example, my mother, I think, wanted to outdistance a sibling. [Dear Abby is Ann Landers's sister.] It was important for her to get ahead of her sister. My father needed to be rich to be somebody, to have his own identity. He was a poor kid on the streets of a big city, and it got in his head that's how you get away from there—you become rich.

"There's not that kind of motivation with any of my kids. Plus—this is a very antifeminist thing to say—two of my children are girls. You know, working is not, so far as I know, an issue for them, or going to be. Maybe a little more for them than for me. It was never suggested to me that I do anything.

"What would I like my son to become? That's interesting. I don't do that. I'm not that kind of Jewish mother. Whatever he is geared for, he should do it and enjoy. Although my kid has said to me, 'You know I know what it means when Grandma says you'd be a good doctor.' He says, 'I know what that means.'

"Some rich families I believe handle their kids very destructively on money. There's a very rich family here, I mean really rich. And one of the grandchildren, a kid about ten, of the man who made the money, came home one day from school in about the fourth or fifth grade and said to his mother, 'Are we rich?' And she said, 'Yes we are, but it doesn't count because Grandpa made all the money.' I mean, look what she did to the kid's father. That story has always stayed with me.

"The kid now sees his father as a shmuck. What the mother was saying was, 'Don't worry, honey, it's Grandpa's money. You know we've got it, but it has nothing to do with us, and your father never accomplished anything.'

"Talk about my kids and my worries. My son, who has a marvelous mind, is somehow into the idea of the value of money, which thrills me. One day he was going to visit a friend, when he was young, on the bus. It was Sunday and I said, 'I think it's cheaper today—it's Sunday. Hang around and I'll check.' I called the bus company and I was right. He says, 'Okay, Mom, but the call cost you at least twenty cents.' There's hope for a kid like that, I think.

"To me, money has special meaning in my work as a writer. Not that I need it, but it's a yardstick of how I'm doing. I just signed a deal which to my knowledge is the highest in this field for the kind of work I'm going to do and how often I'm going to do it. It was important to me not to get had. It shouldn't matter that I have a lot of money to live on. If I'm good and they want me, they can pay, because that's how I know I'm good.

"I went to a psychiatrist for a time. She said I had much insecurity and craziness about money. I know from working with her that to me money was always a sign of acceptance, love, worth, affection. If you were worth it, you would somehow be given or get a lot of money. In other words, money to me has always been a symbol of self-worth."

GROWING UP WEALTHY

In Margo's money talk she touched upon a number of issues at the crux of the experience of being rich in America. One of the most interesting of her comments, I think, relates to her learning about her family fortune, her parents' ruse and her relief when she learned of it. It sounds as if wealthy parents have to face a day of fiscal reckoning, dropping some kind of bomb on their kids *vis à vis* the family net worth. What could be so bad about such good news?

The problem wealthy parents face is imparting to their children just how wealthy and privileged they are without robbing them of motivation in the bargain. After all, a primary purpose of work is to support oneself financially. If supporting oneself is unnecessary, why work at all?

Children of wealthy parents are more apt to be shielded from the world's realities. Their life struggles are different. Automatically handed wealthy status, in many cases they have no concept of what it's like to be poor. The rags-to-riches mogul is apt to have a much better money sense and understanding of the steps to earning money than his children. The person who originally accumulated the wealth tends to know more about the realities of life at all levels than the person who is handed the wealth.

As one wealthy mother asked me, "What do you tell a ten-year-old boy who is going to inherit $10 million when he's eighteen?" His growing awareness that he doesn't have to work can become problematic because children like this have limited motivation to develop their human skills. Later in life they run the real risk of feeling empty, unaccomplished, and useless despite their money.

A well-known movie star agonized over this issue. "It's tough to bring up kids today in a home where there's lots of money. My sixteen-year-old son is into cars and girls. You know what he talks to me about? Ferraris and Masseratis! I tell him that my first car was a beat-up secondhand Ford, but that makes no impression on him. I try to instill values in him. I'll suggest that he buy an old car and fix it up himself, but he's not interested in restoration. It's got to be new, shiny, and fast. He knows I make plenty of money and he isn't interested in working to buy a car or fixing up an old one. He wants what he wants right then and there. He thinks he's entitled to all these things for doing nothing!"

Most rich kids expect to live on the same scale as their parents. They derive their level of aspiration from what they see around them. And just as poverty can deflate self-esteem, wealth can inflate it. Rich kids can feel arrogant, entitled to financial rewards and at the same time disinterested in the "hard work" responsible for those benefits.

The difficulty in understanding the steps of succeeding and making transitions in the developmental process is called dysgradia, according to Dr. James Wixen, author of *Children of the Rich*.[1] How does a parent *cure* spoiled children with a deficiency in motivation?

Dr. Roy Grinker, Jr. studied the children of the superrich and found them difficult to treat because of the diabolical trio of narcissistic character, parent deprivation, and unusual wealth. His research suggested the best treatment combined emotional counseling, a good maternal surrogate, and ego-strengthening measures.[2]

Marjorie Merriweather Post's father Charles, the cereal king, is one example of a father who successfully raised his child despite enormous assets. When Marjorie was just a girl of ten, he took her to board meetings. She grew up with a grasp of great affairs and became the director of General Foods and for a time mistress of the United States Embassy in the Soviet Union. Paralleling her ambitious and successful professional development, she developed a personal lifestyle that has seldom been matched for its opulence in recent times.

Another interesting case is the Rockefellers. John D., the self-made millionaire, inculcated his offspring with a sense of the responsibilities of wealth. His sons, David R., Nelson, and Winthrop, were active in public philanthropy and public service as well, the latter two serving as governors of New York and Arkansas, respectively. Succeeding generations behaved in a variety of ways to the family fortune, from shunning it to following traditional paths.

Being born into a wealthy family, and raising children within a family of substantial means, has a peculiar challenge all its own. Carly Simon, singer and songwriter, emerged from the publishing clan (half of Simon and Schuster) to say this about her personal money struggles: "At twenty-one I received a huge sum of money from a trust fund. During the next five years, psychiatry bills consumed most of it. I was into a lot of self-destructive trips then and I needed help. I had a nervous breakdown when I was nineteen. In my early twenties I was still in bad shape. I paid all that money and still didn't get myself straightened out. I stopped therapy for a while. When I was twenty-seven I started seeing a psychiatrist again. The second time I was in better shape. I just wasn't moving ahead, but eventually I was able to. People look at me and say, 'She has everything.' They don't know what I've been through to get where I am, to maintain what I am."

AFFLUENZA

John Levy, Director of San Francisco's Carl Jung Institute, coined the term "affluenza" to refer to the problems many people have coping with inherited wealth. In a five-year study of people who have inherited wealth, Levy found that the price of wealth can be crippling because of emotional and psychological fears, feelings of isolation, and impotence, and, ironically, a sense of worthlessness. An environment of nannies and servants, where the stresses of earning a living are not present, can in effect become a "golden ghetto" in which children fail to mature intellectually and emotionally.

Apparently the biggest obstacle of all to rich people in the grips of affluenza is the feeling that they don't deserve help with their problems. According to Levy, "Many rich people believe that they don't have the right to have problems. They often feel ashamed of complaining. There is an incredible loneliness at the top."[3]

It is hard for most people on the lower rungs of the financial ladder to sympathize with the rich who feel victimized by their wealth, paranoid about being seen as a walking dollar bill, incapable of spending their fortunes, choosing self-denial or escape from family privilege and status. In the final analysis, it's all relative, and while affluent victims may not need a telethon to raise aid, they do need self-help groups to help them cope and help them distribute some of their fortune to worthy causes. Organizations like the Crossroads Fund in Chicago and New York's Funding Exchange help in getting some of the weight off their backs.

SUDDENLY ACQUIRED WEALTH

Sudden wealth is another interesting arena. For example: How do lottery winners cope? Feelings of shock, glee, and freedom often give way to other not so happy feelings and experiences. Another finding of John Levy's study was that people who inherit large sums often seek anonymity and become suspicious of their friends' motives, and sometimes need psychiatric counseling. My studies found similar results, so much so that it brings to mind St. Teresa's maxim—later popularized by Truman Capote—that more tears are shed over answered prayers than over unanswered ones.

Take the case of Rosa who won $600,000 in a lottery. "People are so mean. I didn't know people could be so mean. You have no idea. It can be miserable." She says her troubles began when her address was printed in the paper. She relates in a halting voice that her father is worried about her, and that her nerves have never been so upset. She rambles on about so many thugs in the street, trying to be a religious person, living like she always lived, alluding to the fear and uncertainty her windfall has brought. "I'll just have to leave," she says of job, neighborhood, and family, and finishes up with "I just hope you win the lottery and see what happens to you!"

Staff Sergeant Michael McIntyre, Andrews Air Force Base, winner of over a million says, "I got my phone number changed twice. I'd get calls. People would always be knocking on my door. I knew it wasn't a friend of mine at four in the morning. I'd get mail from kooks, letters from off-the-wall causes. Somebody wanted me to contribute to UFO research; somebody was asking for bail money. I got letters from jail— I'm-not-guilty pleas. I've eight more months to go in the service, then I have the definite incentive to get out."

Big lottery winners inherit a period of adjustment that is highly stressful and a lifestyle often foreign to them. A British study of 191 pool winners found that 70 percent were lonelier as a result of giving up work and changing neighborhoods, because of their winning large sums of money.

Of course, sudden wealth isn't always a hardship. One study of twenty-two big-time lottery winners found no difference between their degree of happiness and that of ordinary people. Curt Gentry co-author of *Helter Skelter,* the book on Charles Manson he wrote with Vincent Bugliosi, commented: "It's hard to believe what has happened! Everything good that can happen to a book happened to *Helter-Skelter.* It was originally contracted with Putnam. After I'd gone through the advance and nearly three years into the book, they turned it down because the Manson case was no longer topical. W. W. Norton picked it up and their enthusiasm charged me during the last phase of writing. The next thing, the Book-of-the-Month Club took it. It sold 200,000 in trade, 200,000 in book club, and 6,000,000 in paperback, and was bought for a four-hour TV show.

"As it unfolded, the whole thing seemed unreal to me. It still is. In selling paperback rights, we were thinking in terms of $250,000. Bantam bid $771,000. Things like that, if you never had any real money, are unreal. I actually had to pinch myself, hoping I hadn't hallucinated the whole thing.

"I bought a mansion. It's a beautiful wood house, rosewood walls, teak floors, walnut bannisters, something that I've always wanted. I gave up my 65 Ford for a new Mercedes. I thought when I came into a lot of money I would just lie back and play with it—manage it, treat it, and stop writing altogether. But my work habits are too strong. I went to Hawaii for a two-week honeymoon—after the first week I was itching to get back to the typewriter."

Entertainers, especially actors, are often on a roller-coaster ride with wealth. Telly Savalas commented after his success with Kojak: "I spend my money, baby! Success in this business comes and goes, and I know I ain't gonna be on top forever, so I'm having a good time while I'm here.

"As a kid, I was rich one day and the next day my brothers and I were out in the street with shoeshine boxes. So I see the ups and downs and don't trust any of it. So I'm having a good time.

"I'm spending all of it. On what? Nothing bizarre, nothing mad. I spend to help other people, people who are down. I bought a horse, and so far won half a million with him. Some investment, huh? My buddy and I are going to build a private club with an exclusive membership, so exclusive I don't think he and I are gonna let ourselves become members. You gotta own horses to get in. The whole thing's on paper now."

EARNED WEALTH

Nolan Bushnell, creator of video electronic games and devices and Chairman of the Board of Atari, Inc., had the following viewpoint on financial success as it relates to personal fulfillment: "Being successful is kind of dull once you get there. The major change in my life is, basically, I have less time to enjoy myself. Before developing Pong and creating this company, I was a $1000-a-month engineer and all I ever wanted to do was get together a quarter of a million someday, invest it, and be a bum, traveling around for the rest of my life. Well, now I've got lots more money and I'm able to accomplish what I always thought I wanted, but I've decided against it. It turned out that my work was just too much fun. I work twelve, fourteen hours a day and it's a real challenge, a lot of interesting people, interesting things to do, making decisions that make things happen. I love it!

"The thing that amazes me is just how really few things there are to spend your money on. I bought a motorcycle, a boat, a good stereo. The only bizarre thing I've done is develop a game collection in my house— old board games, old pinball machines. I've got one that dates back to 1906, pre-coin machine. We've set aside a room for games and the collection is growing all the time."

THE NEW AMERICAN MILLIONAIRES

According to 1989 statistics, with inflation in part paving the way, the American collection of millionaires is growing. In Los Angeles alone, which now boasts the highest degree of American affluence, 3 percent of the population or 160,000 millionaires have taken up residence. What's more astounding is how fast wealth is accumulating. The California Franchise Tax board reported that 1 percent of filers earned $100,000 in 1980. By 1985, Los Angeles County boasted 2.1 percent, a 100 percent increase in assets. With wealth growing at this accelerated rate, the number of millionaires, if not billionaires, is bound to rise enormously by the twenty-first century.

How did all these millionaires make it? According to bank industry figures, 37 percent were self-employed entrepreneurs who struck gold in an opportunistic marketplace; 31 percent were incorporated business persons; 16 percent were employees of firms; and 12 percent retired; a collection of Beverly Hills doctors, restaurateurs, and ad agency owners.

Many important millionaires in America are really billionaires when the inflation of their holdings are taken into account. According to Forbes, in 1989 there were fifty-five American billionaires. Most of them, unlike billionaires Donald Trump and the newly crowned Merv Griffin, now seem to prefer anonymity and resist the flamboyant display of their wealth that Thorstein Veblen wrote about in his classic 1899 book, *The Theory of the Leisure Class.*

Following are four portraits of prototypical publicity-resistant billionaires who remain relatively unknown to the general public.

Paul Mellon:

The only one of our portraits with a legendary name of the stature of historic dynasties like the Fords, Morgans, and Rockefellers, Mellon was educated at Choate, Yale, and Cambridge, and on the Board of Directors of Mellon National Corporation. He chose to spend his life not accumulating further fortunes but distributing family wealth. The challenge he set for himself—"to spend it sensibly"—has been accomplished with every bit as much style and organizational flair as his father demonstrated in making the Mellon millions. Since World War II, his family and their foundation have given away more than $1 billion to universities, art museums, wild-life sanctuaries, historical societies, and mental health programs. Of course, he lived elegantly in a variety of homes in Virginia, Washington, New York, Cape Cod, and Antigua, in the company of a renowned art collection and championship thoroughbred horses, but his lifestyle demonstrated a work ethic. As he said, "Giving away large sums of money is a soul-searching problem. You can cause as much damage with it as you may do good."

Ray Kroc:

The late Ray Kroc is another example of the working billionaire. At seventy-three he was still touring McDonald franchises making certain parking lots were litter-free and managers were doing their jobs. He started out selling a malted milk machine capable of turning out six drinks at once. When a San Bernadino hamburger stand ordered eight in 1954, he delivered personally and never left. He convinced transplanted New Englanders Richard and Maurice McDonald to franchise, and bought them out in 1961 for $2.7 million. The estimated value of the company rose to over $1 billion. In his lifetime, Kroc bought a 210-acre California ranch, a 6000-square-foot apartment on Lake Shore Drive in Chicago, four helicopters, a ninety-foot yacht, a Fort Lauderdale beach house, and a baseball team. However, his ruling obsession was the company. Golden arches were everywhere, even in his cuff links, tie bars, on his rings, and embroidered on his jackets. His widow carries on his tradition of helping charitable causes. And now, with the Golden Arches spreading its burgers across Russia and other eastern European countries, the sky is the limit.

John Donald MacArthur:

MacArthur eschews all the conventional trappings of wealth. He started out in insurance at seventeen and by the mid-1950s controlled a dozen firms. A mortgage failure dumped 6000 acres of prime Palm Beach, Florida, real estate into his lap and, knowing a good thing, he jumped eagerly into the Florida land boom, eventually becoming that state's biggest landowner. His assets from insurance companies like Bankers Life and Casualty Co. skirt $802 million, and he owns banks and hotels, too.

"I used to have a big house," he says of his Chicago residence, "but when I'd go away on trips, the yardman would let the grass grow and the servants would drink up my Scotch. We do better living in a hotel."

Daniel Keith Ludwig:

Ludwig is worth $3 billion amassed from tanker fleets, real estate, timber, cattle breeding, rice, and mining rare minerals, much of this on a 3.5-million-acre Brazilian estate. This is a far cry from the nine-year-old Michigan boy who bought a sunken twenty-six-foot boat for $25, repaired it, and rented it out. His business acumen paid off. In the mid-30s he struck it rich with a simple, audacious financing scheme: Before buying or building a tanker, he would negotiate a long-term charter with a major oil company, then use his charter as collateral for a bank loan which would cover the tanker's cost. By pyramiding such deals, he built up an armada of fifty ships without investing a cent of his own money, and thus amassed his billions.

A New York admirer of Ludwig's said at one point, "He's seventy-nine going on forty" because at that age he was still walking from his Fifth Avenue penthouse each morning to his office to see his business holdings—coal mines in West Virginia and Australia, a $400,000 oil refinery under construction in Scotland, a 10,000-acre orange plantation in Panama, and a string of luxury hotels including the Acapulco Princess in Mexico. With an international schedule of such assets and responsibilities, it's no wonder he has little time, according to friends, for yachts, girlfriends, private planes—the things one might associate with someone of great wealth.

The billionaires just described reflect the national trend that working, not leisure, delivers maximum pleasure for people, even the superwealthy. Never before have there been so many with so much money who have so few hours to sit back and enjoy their leisure pursuits. It does seem that many of the rich, even the superrich, are leading ordinary lives in an extraordinary tax bracket.

There are some exceptions, however, who still practice the kind of conspicuous consumption described by Thorstein Veblen in his classic 1899 book, *The Theory of the Leisure Class*. For such people, mere possession of great wealth isn't enough of a distinction. It needs to be displayed, and displayed lavishly. Mansions, travel, adventures, and festivities are the mediums conveying the message of opulence and affluence.

A prime example of conspicuous consumption is the much admired and much envied New York billionaire Donald Trump. He is clearly an Insatiable. When asked if he had ever thought of psychotherapy, Trump replied, "No, I've never felt even close to needing it. I haven't felt I was ever out of control. I keep busy. I don't have time to think about my problems."[4]

On many matters related to money, Trump's responses are illuminating:

"Who has done as much as I have? No one has done more in New York than me." [And onward to L.A. in the 1990s.]

"I love to have enemies. I fight my enemies. I like beating my enemies to the ground."

"My style of deal-making is quite simple and straightforward. I just keep pushing and pushing and pushing to get what I'm after."

"Those who dislike me don't know me, and have never met me. My guess is that they dislike me out of jealousy."

"I like thinking big. If you're going to be thinking anyway, you might as well think big."

"Nobody pushes me around, you understand? I don't want to do it [litigation], but nobody is going to push me around."

"A little more moderation would be good. Of course, my life hasn't exactly been one of moderation."

At six foot two, real estate tycoon Donald J. (for John) Trump does not really loom colossus-high above the horizon of New York and New Jersey. He has created no great work of art or ideas, and even as a maker or possessor of money he does not rank among the top ten in America. In his forties, he has seized a large fistful of that contemporary coin known as celebrity. There has been artfully hyped talk about his having political ambitions, worrying about nuclear proliferation, even someday running for President. No matter how far-fetched that may be, something about his combination of blue-eyed swagger and success has caught the public fancy and made him in many ways a symbol of an acquisitive and mercenary age.

Although Trump's financial power has been cyclical with some severe downturns he remains notorious in the public eye. He worries about people really knowing what he's about. As he put it: "When you start studying yourself too deeply, you may see something you don't want to see. Once people figure you out, you're in big trouble."

Another man who flaunted his wealth when he was on top was Bernard Cornfeld, who is certainly a millionaire if not a billionaire. He acquired his riches from the now defunct worldwide business, International Overseas Investments. This once-billion-dollar investment firm was in part gutted by the mysterious superwealthy Robert Vesco, who in the 1960s allegedly stole $200 million from the corporation and bought himself the nation of Costa Rica.

Cornfeld as former head of the firm came out of the same debacle with an unknown fortune. He lives in luxury in his mansion in Beverly Hills, maintains a castle in France, and a townhouse in London. Cornfeld's luxurious life has been notorious because of his playboy lifestyle, which has for at least twenty years notably incorporated a harem of beautiful women.

Prior to our meeting, I had acquainted myself with his past involvements as head of International Overseas Investments. The rise of Investors Overseas Services (IOS) and its creator Bernie Cornfeld was the success story of international finance in the 1960s, proof that American-style capitalism could be extended to the world at large.

From a modest start in Paris in 1956 selling mutual funds to servicemen, IOS grew into a financial colossus, gathering from every corner of the globe a hoard of risk capital and the savings of innumerable individuals. Its rise paralleled the boom market of the 1960s; its fall, the market collapse of the 1970s. The crash of the $2.4 billion organization shook many of the most august financial institutions of the Western World at that time.

I interviewed Mr. Cornfeld in his Beverly Hills "castle," a Gothic mansion, turrets and all, where a Rolls-Royce, an Excalibur, and a Mercedes stood guard. The mansion's interior was equally impressive, lavishly decorated with fine antiques, paintings, Oriental rugs, and assorted ladies-in-waiting, who appeared and vanished from the room during the interview.

"When I was a boy in Istanbul, the city of my birth, my father was a reasonably old man. The house basements in Istanbul were lit at the time by metal grates. My father was walking along the street over one, it collapsed, and he fell down two flights. He was in the hospital for a long time, had some surgery, but after that accident he never really recovered. He had to walk with a cane and had a permanent limp.

"One of my earliest recollections about money was the fact that my father would, in the process of walking down the street, watch where he put his cane. When he went out, there was almost never an occasion when he didn't come back with the equivalent of pennies, nickels, and dimes that he picked up in the course of his walk. I was startled with the quantity of coins that he found. He would fill up small banks. I became impressed with the fact at an early age that anyone who happened to be looking for money tended to find it.

"The other early recollection I have about money began in Brooklyn. Because we had very little money, my allowance was lower than that of my friends. It consisted of a nickel a week. It's hard to believe, but on the basis of a nickel a week, I would save money. I had very few things to spend money on, except candy. And my father would always buy large boxes of candy, so it was given to me for free. I put my meager savings into a little piggybank. When I started working as a grocery delivery boy, and later as an age guesser at Coney Island, I was struck with the fact that once you got beyond the point of having what you needed for subsistence—just paying for groceries, eating, and the like—money really took on a very different kind of importance, and for me it was a very secondary importance.

"In my adult life I made relatively huge amounts of money and in the process I really wasn't very much concerned with the money. I was more concerned with what I was doing—the drama, the importance, the excitement that one of the end results was going to be making X-amount of money.

"I began my adult career, strange as it may sound, as a social worker. I have a Master of Social Work degree from Columbia University.

"I grew up in an area of New York that was predominantly radical. My own inclination was with the Socialist Party. I had trouble getting a job in social work and a friend in the mutual fund business turned me on to it. It seemed to me that there was an ingredient in the mutual fund business that was tantamount to a kind of people's capitalism in that it provided a way, short of nationalization, which would give poor people a chance to earn money with money. I thought that the mutual fund business was a way in which, say, the average taxi driver could share in and benefit from the fruits of the capitalist system, much in the same way that a capitalist would, and that it permitted him to create wealth.

"Early in my business, we did a statistical study that I thought was kind of interesting at the time. We found that if anyone invested a dollar a day, which was something that was feasible to almost anybody even back in 1925, in any one of the existing open-end mutual funds over a period of forty years [which were the productive periods of anyone's life], they would have invested a total of, oh, [a little over] $13,000—$360 a year, $3600 in ten years, and so on. The end result of this process was that, at the end of a forty-year period, the investor would have been worth something like a quarter of a million dollars!

"Now that really meant anyone with no feel for the market, the economy, or investments, had the possibility of creating what by most standards would be considered a substantial amount of wealth simply by becoming a part of our investment system.

"That notion seemed so staggering to me, I had them redo the studies, put them through computers and fool with them in all kinds of ways. With the worst investment, all anyone could end up with was a quarter of a million in forty years. That impressed me.

"It meant that there was a painless way of achieving an economic revolution. The economic revolution would produce a social revolution—a nonviolent, painless kind that could solve a lot of human problems. I believed you could relieve some of the social problems with the monetary system I created. My socialist inclinations had me convinced that any company I founded would have to be the kind in which anybody contributing should have the right to a piece. And so I developed a corporate stock option plan which worked as a very effective incentive. It permitted my associates in the company, especially those who were with me early in the game, to end up owning more than 80 percent by 1969.

"We had a public underwriting which diluted my ownership considerably, even though I received about $8 million. The end result was once we were public, stock prices began to go down. Stockholders became panicky. One day they saw the paper value of the stock worth $30 million, the next day $24 million. They saw themselves losing one, two, three million a day. These paper losses were not particularly significant to me, but people's psychology was. We brought in a board of directors to solve our problems. They took in Robert Vesco.

"Once he took control, he got rid of all the fiduciary institutions. The Credit Suisse held all of the fund's cash, the Bank of New York all securities. Then he replaced Credit Suisse with a bank he fully controlled and Bank of New York with a small New Jersey bank with whom he had close relations. He drained off as much cash as he could steal. There was an indictment, but his contributions to Nixon helped free him. He bought the little republic of Costa Rica.

"I came out OK, but the little investors lost everything. When I realized that almost all the money had been stolen by Vesco, I felt horrible. All those years of work, the excitement turned to rubble, creating pain and sorrow for people; that was the most dismal and depressing point in my life. Watching my little company grow from a handful of people to 25,000 salespersons, an organization managing $2.5 billion, half a dozen insurance companies, five banks, eighteen mutual funds—to see it all crash was very painful.

"There were a lot of people I was disappointed in, a lot I was proud of in the fight. In the end, you are alone, that has been my experience.

"On the happy side, one of the nice things about being rich is that you're reputed to have an element of brilliance. Because people assume that brilliance, often it emerges. Certainly, people pay more attention to what you say.

"My wealth has enabled me to act out a childhood fantasy. It was a King Arthur fantasy where I rescued fair maidens and was the lord of the castle. I am still living out my fantasy. I've always had houses that look like castles. One of the five I've owned was a hundred-year-old castle in France at the headwaters of the Rhine River. It had towers, a moat, and a drawbridge. I would ride my horse through the countryside and imagine it was five hundred years ago and this was my chateau. I would like to have worn the costumes.

"The lord [of the manor] also had certain rights . . . the chateau's virgins. It's no secret that women are attracted to money and power. If there's only money, you just get a limited kind of woman, a money-oriented boob. I expect something more from a woman than simply sex. There have been a lot of women around me all my life. It never mattered to me all that much, but there are a whole lot of women attracted primarily to the climate of wealth, only secondarily to me. These women were not around for very long. Of course, I don't think there were any who were totally oblivious to my money. . . . I've given women a lot of money—but not nearly as much as I've given to lawyers.

"There is an element of pursuit in my relationship with women. They are always around in quantity and variety. I think probably right now there are about twelve women in the house. Four or five come to dinner every night, and some of them stay. I started living with a multiplicity of women about ten years ago. I came to the conclusion that the one-to-one relationship has two possible fates: monotony or a sort of psychological dependency. I wanted to avoid both. I wanted relationships to stay fresh and good. I found the only way for that to happen was to be involved with many women simultaneously.

"I keep running into people who tell me they became jaded at forty. I've never been bored with sex for one minute.

"I'm convinced that what Fitzgerald said was right, that the only difference between the rich and the poor is that the rich have money. I don't think there are any qualities that distinguish the rich from the poor. And the only thing that distinguishes the rich from one another is the degree of insecurity about their money. The old rich are more comfortable with their money. The nouveau riches live in fear that it will all disappear tomorrow, or next week, or next year. I'm nouveau riche."

Nouveau riche or not, Bernie Cornfeld seems to be living out more than one fantasy, and some eccentricities afforded the rich. His is hardly a hard-luck tale, or an ordinary one.

In the process of researching the super-wealthy, I also interviewed many "ordinary" millionaires, who were not as flamboyant about their wealth as the Trumps and Cornfeld. The following summaries reveal their stories of wealth..

Joan, a forty-nine year-old homemaker:

"Money means a lot to me. It means freedom, independence. It means I can do what I want when I want to do it. To me, money is really a joy—the spice of life. I'm thankful I've had the opportunity to enjoy money and what it brings without having to kill myself in search of it.

"Since I married Howard, life has been one big vacation. We have already seen virtually every stretch of the world but Russia and China. We've never been on safari in Africa, but we've done just about everything else—Europe seventeen times, Austria for two years.

"Howard was vice-president of his father's company when we married, and eleven years later, president. Our son will take over in five years. That is when our money will really pay big dividends because we are going to take a leisurely trip around the world."

Harry, a fifty-one-year-old building contractor:

"Money is everything to me. I can go places and do things I never dreamed I would be able to do when I was a kid. I just got back from Europe. My business runs itself, and I have enough money in the bank so I'll never have to worry. I have to thank the American system for all this. If I lived anywhere else, I'd be killing myself in the hot sun till I keeled over.

"The day I became a millionaire was the happiest day of my life. My accountant told me I was worth a million. I threw a gigantic party and gave all my crews the day off. It probably cost $15,000, but it was worth it. When you've got a million bucks, you feel safe and secure. At least I've always felt safe and secure since that day."

Don, forty-nine:

Don is a multimillionaire from various business enterprises, but hardly a happy one. Don changed his name to disassociate himself from his religion and family background. His wife is ill, residing in a rest home. His two sons have left home. Don grinds on with his work.

"No slave laboring under the whip of the slave driver ever worked harder than me. I pride myself on what I consider an enormous capacity for work. I have nothing but scorn for those who, in their eyes, feel they are not wasting time. I consider my success mainly due to my stressing efficiency, my meticulous attention to detail, and my iron constitution. I see no pleasure in doing anything but making money. I seek no hobbies or other activities that would waste my time. I have a lot of pressures in this business, I sometimes do not even have the time to sleep. I spend all night thinking about the business.

"I'm in analysis. I go regularly, but it hasn't helped much. I enjoy a big score in my real estate business more than an insight. I promise myself constantly to work less, but I can't seem to do it. I just keep on overworking. It's fantastic!"

Don sounds like the Gordon Gecco insatiable type of millionaire of the "greed-is-good" school as depicted in the movie "Wall Street" (1988). Money is his life's blood. Everything else—recreation, love, family, hobbies, contentment—pales by comparison.

As you can see from all this rich money talk, the rich are a varied breed. Some have problems, some make problems for themselves, some have no problems; it all depends on how they view and use or abuse their wealth. The one generalization that can be made is that it's difficult to make too many generalizations about the super-rich— except they are different because they have more freedom and power.

7

The High Cost of Poverty

*T*HE STOCK market crash of 1929 and the Great Depression that followed etched a lasting, haunting impression upon the American psyche. No one lived through it unscathed. But, as Will Rogers, a perceptive humorist and social commentator, pointed out in 1931, "The poor paid a higher price than the wealthy."

He said, "There is not an unemployed man in the country who hasn't contributed to the wealth of every millionaire in America. The working classes didn't bring this on, it was the big boys who thought the financial drunk was going to last forever, and overbought, overmerged, and over capitalized. . .

"We've got more wheat, more corn, more food, more cotton, more money in the banks, more everything in the world than any nation that ever lived ever had, yet we are starving to death. We are the first nation in the history of the world to go to the poorhouse in an automobile."

Rogers believed the greedy rich were responsible for the epidemic of poverty that swept across America in the 1930s, and his viewpoint may portend and explain the fall which may emerge from the senseless corporate takeovers, the savings and loan lootings, and the junk bond fiascoes we are attempting to resolve in the 1990s.

When it comes to poverty, the question of who's to blame always pops up. Are the poor and homeless victims of their own sloth, of lack of economic opportunity, or of emotional problems, or, given our economic system, does a segment of the population fall between the cracks? Regardless of who or what is to blame for poverty in America, and how much culpability goes where in the system, poverty does indeed have a price tag, a toll exacted in raw emotional currency. And it is a high price to pay. As you listen to my interviews with poor people, you will get a clearer picture of the emotional costs of being poor in our affluent society.

In 1988, statistician George Gallup polled ten thousand people in seventy countries about their finances, and concluded: "It was hoped that somewhere we'd find a country whose people are poor but happy. We found no such place."

Marilyn was not a Depression child, but she shares the experience of poverty and its legacy. Just as the Depression scarred a nation forever, Marilyn's poverty turned out to be inescapable. Marilyn is an attractive, forty-year-old woman, reasonably successful, and married to a business-man who earns $100,000 a year. Despite this, her past haunts her present life. As a child she was impoverished not only financially but emotionally. She became a drug addict, but had now been clean for fifteen years. As she put it, "Drugs buried my feelings of being poor and nobody." At the time I interviewed her, she was living a happier, more productive life than she had as a child.

"I remember lots of family fights about money. I remember money being hidden in light fixtures and under mattresses. My mother, big and fat, kept money hidden in her undergarments, which she showed me in the outdoor toilet when I was six.

"I remember my father's and mother's constant money battles. 'You get out.' 'Give me some money and I will.' 'I'm not giving you no f— ing money.' Back and forth.

"She would hide money from him, take money from him, and then the two of us would leave him. But then times would be very, very hard because without him supporting us she'd have to get a job as a waitress. And that was why she left me with my grandmother for a year, because she couldn't afford to keep me.

"Another thing I remember from my poor childhood is that my folks would drink and they used to go to beer joints and bars. Sometimes they would take me with them and they would stand me up on the bar and have me sing or dance. And these drunks would throw money and give me pennies and stuff.

"I thought it was terrific. I was getting a little attention.

"I guess what was really bad was when I was in love with this boy and my father wouldn't allow him in our house. We didn't have any money between us. I mean, we were just walking around starving half the time. We couldn't even get a hamburger or anything. We didn't have a car. We didn't have anything. So in order to get something to eat we used to walk ten miles to his house. Sometimes it was raining and stormy and the gutters were full of water, and he'd be carrying me, and we'd get there and all there'd be in his house to eat would be cereal or something. There were five kids in his family. So we had a really hard time. We couldn't afford to go to the movies. Fortunately, we were crazy about each other sexually, so we just made love a lot.

"Our lives were really hard. And it was terrible when he got arrested for stealing a car. It was after my father beat me up and he still worked hard to try and get me away from my folks. There was no bail money to get him out of jail or anything. So you know, when you're poor you're just totally helpless. Anybody can do anything to you and you're just a total victim. You have no choice.

"When I was in high school, all the other girls had nice clothes and I didn't. One girl I remember, Sharon, lived in a big white house with columns. She wore cashmere sweaters, dressed really nice, and was very popular. I just didn't have any decent clothes. I went to school looking really shabby a lot of the time. I didn't fit in. My mother and I lived in this girl's back garage apartment. It was crummy. There was one bed and there wasn't even a bedroom or anything.

"I remember graduation, I heard Sharon's mother say, 'Well you've got to invite her. She lives right in back,' and she said, 'I don't want to invite that creep,' or something like that. 'No, she's weird.' I forget what it was, but she really didn't want me to come to her graduation party. And it was all because she was rich and I was poor.

"In my case, being poor was combined with ignorance. I saw a lot of movies when I was a kid. Sometimes my parents might be in the bar and they would let me go to the movies. That changed my life. I saw rich people with good taste. I noticed in movies that most people ate at nice tables and had tablecloths. You know, there'd be some young, beautiful girl sweeping down a stairway with her gown trailing behind her. It was all very lovely and very formal. Meanwhile, we were living in a trailer, and eating out of cans; you know, fried Spam and potatoes. We never sat down and had a nice meal with candlelight and napkins. It was unheard of. We ate like a bunch of animals compared to the rich people I saw in the movies."

Marilyn's present state of mind is still ruled by money. She's emotionally impoverished. She's envious of others' wealth, resentful even though she herself now has substantial means. People like Marilyn, with pasts stained with deprivation, grow into adults who still feel deprived. Money was an overly significant factor in their early lives. They perceived it as a medium of love and approval. As adults, they continually try to extract more money from others, and seem incapable of obliterating their continuing feelings of living in poverty.

POOR CHILDREN

The fact that poverty often carries an emotional stigma akin to some psychic taboo makes it all the more difficult to hear stories about the emotional impact of poverty on children. According to 1988 Census Bureau figures, a child under eighteen is three times as likely to wind up in the 33 million pool of poverty. These children are destined to have a childhood of hunger, abuse, crime, drugs, and terror.

The following interviews describe the experience of poverty from children's points of view.

Wyoma, age fourteen:

Wyoma is a black girl whose father has disappeared from the family situation. "I've had a lot of bad experiences because we don't have money. I don't want you to think that we haven't eaten just because we don't have any food in the refrigerator right now. Momma's been good to us, but there just isn't a way to feed all of us on relief checks. And we don't get our check until tomorrow.

"Most of the time things are pretty good around here. Of course, we have to fight for everything we get, but we've been raised to expect that. I think the worst time we ever had was about two years ago when Momma was really sick—too sick to move her. None of the neighbors wanted to help. Anyway, she needed a doctor real bad, but no doctor would come. She had a terrible fever and all, and I thought she was going to die for sure.

"So I stayed up with her for three days until she got over the fever. If we had some money we could have got her into a hospital. We could have at least paid a taxi driver. Ambulance drivers don't like coming down here. My momma almost died that time.

"That was about the worst experience. All the time we're scraping to get two meals a day. We can't afford three meals a day like most folks, but we can usually pay for two meals for everybody. The worst about that is when my little brothers, Henry and Chester, don't get something to eat. Seeing them hurting so much, so little and unable to help themselves, hurts me.

"I have stolen to get food. I'll never stop to think about it as long as someone in my family is hungry. The store owners are making plenty of money. They don't need their food as much as we do. My Momma says they got plenty of money and they overcharge us.

"There is nothing as important as money. No matter how good we are down here, we don't have a chance because we don't have money. The only way to beat it is to take to the streets or to get out. There's no way an honest person can make a living in this neighborhood.

"I'll admit it, my older sister hustles for money. If it wasn't for her dropping ten or twenty dollars on us once in a while, we would be worse off than we are. She gives most of her money to her pimp, but she sneaks some in here.

"What about me? Well, I've thought about it. And sometimes I think why not? I'm no angel—and I think why give it away when I can make some good bread. My sister ain't hurting. Hustling looks like a better life than the one I got."

Steve, age ten:

Steve's family is not very well off. His parents are both low-income workers.

"I think money is important. It has to be, otherwise my people wouldn't be gone all the time. My dad and mom both work all the time. When they're not working they get drunk a lot. Especially on weekends.

"I ask my dad why he is always drunk and he says 'to forget.' I guess it gets bad in the packing plant, but my teacher says that's no excuse to get drunk. My mom works downtown in a garment factory and she's always complaining about that too, because it's hard work. But she tells me if she didn't work we couldn't have the things we have. I would rather have her at home.

"My people are always talking about how they don't have enough money. If they had more money we could all be happy, but they don't. I want to get a baseball mitt, but I can't have one now because we don't have enough money to buy it.

"I would give anything to get a mitt, but my dad says I'll just have to wait. The most bad thing I think of about money was last Christmas. I got one lousy present. I cried all day on Christmas.

"My mom always says that I have to do good in school. She says if I don't, I am going to end up like her and Dad, poor and working all the time. I don't want to be poor. She says I have to go to college to get a good job. Dad is usually working, but he never went to college, so he couldn't get a good job.

"But it's hard to take when my friends chop me on the arm in school. They all wear pretty cool clothes. I don't always let it bug me when they chop me because I wear old pants from my brother. But sometimes they make me cry. If we had more money I could buy clothes that would be better than theirs. Then I would laugh at them and see how they like it.

"I steal anything I can. It's not that I'm bad. It's because I need stuff. Like, sometimes after school, I get hungry. And I know that I can rip off a couple candy bars at this liquor store.

"If you gave me a thousand dollars, I would go out and buy a new car for my dad, some new dresses for my mom, and some new clothes for me, and a color TV. Then with the money left over I would go shopping and bring back a lot of food. Good stuff like cakes and candies, stuff we don't always have."

POOR PARENTS

An additional burden of growing up poor is growing up with parents who are not constructive role models. Absentee fathers, working mothers and fathers who must be absent much of the time account for some of this. Even more a factor, however, is the poverty mentality itself. Poor adults lead hard lives, mired in their own anger, powerlessness, and frustration. When adults are depressed and overworked, how can they be positive, empathetic parents?

Louise, age twenty-nine:

Lone welfare mother, Louise lives in South Central Los Angeles, a twentieth-century urban war zone. She said: "I had a bastard husband who got up and left three years ago. I've got four little kids. I can't get a steady job because I can't leave them on their own all day. It's hell, man.

"Sure I get some welfare money, but it's not enough to do anything with. I don't like to feel like I'm no good, but that's the way I've been feeling. The kids don't understand what happened either. They're always making things tougher by asking for their daddy. I try to explain it, but they think they caused their daddy to leave. It wasn't their fault and it wasn't my fault. I guess things got too heavy on Henry's back. The easiest way was to leave.

"What would I do for money? You name it. Sure, I've gone down with a lot of men, but what would you do if you were me? For $100 I would make love to anyone—$100 would keep us in groceries for weeks! My values have really changed since Henry left. Before, I tried to be a respectable housewife and mother. I would never think of stealing or ripping off anybody. Henry would've skinned me alive! I was real proud of our family, and I really thought we were going to make it. Then one day he's gone and my whole world was destroyed. Now my attitude toward stealing is totally different. I take anything I can, whenever I can. You've got to have some sort of edge. They don't give me enough money, the only thing I can do is rip the supermarket off here and there to give my kids enough food.

"When you don't have money, it makes the whole world very depressing. It was a real shock to be standing in a welfare line. I always thought welfare was for bad, lazy people who didn't want to work. Then all of a sudden I was on it. I didn't feel like I fit in there, but after a while I got used to it. And I got used to macaroni and hot dogs.

"I've lost touch with my parents. I don't want to shame them. They had such big plans for me. When I was a little girl, they dressed me up like Lena Horne. They wanted me to be a great singer, but when I got older they could see I couldn't sing. I always wanted my parents to be real proud of me, but I know if they could see me now they'd be real disappointed.

"You think money is not important? Money is the only thing that is important. After a while it doesn't matter who you lie to, who you rip off, or what you do to get money. You just know you need the money and that you have to get it from somewhere. A lot of people I know have turned to drinking and dope to ease their problems. I haven't had to do that yet, but it could happen any time. I am doing the best I can, and that's all I can ask of myself."

THE WORKING POOR

The poor usually have less education than those in the middle and upper classes and are apt to work at menial jobs, assembly-line positions, and manual labor. What little money they earn is so critical to their survival that it becomes hyperimportant to them. The poor, unlike other socioeconomic groups, usually work exclusively for money and derive a minimum, if any, emotional satisfaction from their occupations. In my research I found an inverse relationship between education and the importance of money as an occupational aspiration. Those who checked off that money is the only reason they work are overrepresented numerically in the less-than-high-school-education category.

The next several interviews tell what it's like to work at a job you hate just for the money.

Bob, a twenty-seven-year-old spot welder:

"I work to make money. That's the only reason I do this godawful job. I'm on the road two hours a day just to work and back, plus I work eight hours in a loud, hot place that drives me crazy.

"I never had a chance to go to school, because I went into the Navy after high school. I got married right after I got out on Christmas day. I never liked school anyway.

"My parents never really taught me much about money. They were certainly not qualified to teach. My father never paid a bill on time until his sons started supporting him. I kick in and so do my three brothers. That makes a difference to us, but it also makes a big difference for my parents, because for the first time they are able to afford to pay their bills.

"I would steal for the right amount of money, but I would never kill a man for any amount because I would probably be caught, and then I might be sentenced to death. If you could assure me I'd never get caught, I might do it. After all, I've thrown my life away working this stupid job. It would probably be worth the guilt to be able to change my lifestyle.

"Although we've made more this year, I have less buying power. Still, I'm doing as well as anybody else at work. Most of the guys have five or six kids, and they are having real fits. My problems are minor compared to them, but most of these guys are younger too. Most of the guys are lucky to get their house payments paid.

"Although I really love the idea of being rich, I would rather be famous. I would like to be somebody, recognized on the street and in restaurants. Right now I feel like a nobody a lot of the time. Sure I have friends, but none of them are influential.

"I find I am not really happy with my lifestyle now, but I am happier than I was a few years ago. My lifestyle is definitely improving, and I think that tends to make me happier. It sure makes my kids happier because they are able to have some of the things I always wanted but could not afford.

"I think about money almost all the time. The thought of the money I'm making is the only thing that keeps me at work. I really hate that job, but there is nothing I can do about it. So I just put up with it, and wait until I can head back home for a little peace and quiet. I'm always trying to think of new ways to make money, but I haven't thought up any brilliant schemes yet. I am just another blue collar worker, and I have always wanted to be more than that. I rent an apartment and probably will for the rest of my life. I'll never own my own house. Houses in California in a slum begin at $200,000. It's beyond belief!"

Jaoquin, age twenty-three:

Jaoquin works at a car wash in Los Angeles. His financial problems are compounded by his illegal-alien status. "The reason I came to the United States was to make enough money to give my family a better life. I came originally from Ensenada, Mexico. I have five brothers and three sisters. I am the oldest son and my father always wanted me to get out.

"The most depressing thing I can remember is going to bed hungry night after night because my family did not have enough food. I don't want that to happen to my family anymore, and that is why I have come here. I haven't been back home, but I have sent them a little of my earnings. Mostly I have worried about learning English. Now I know it good and I am ready to find a good job.

"My life is much better here than it was in Ensenada. There, we all lived in a one-bedroom house. Often I went to bed hungry, but you learn not to complain. That is just the way it is. I am much happier here in the United States. I share a two-bedroom apartment with five guys. Some might say it is crowded, and by standards here it is. Compared to back home, it is plenty of room. We all came across in the same truck and have remained friends ever since.

"The happiest time was when I got my first money from the car wash. I had to have one of the others cash my check because I had no identification. Money is the reason I do the work I do. I hate drying off cars, but it gets me the money I need. Until I can find something better, it will have to do. But there is no way I would do this work unless I got money for it.

"I have always wanted to make as much as I could, and I would be a much happier man as a rich one than a poor one. I would also be happier being a rich man than a famous man. I would like to be famous for something someday, but I don't know what yet.

"My family is more important than anything in the world. More important than money, for sure. I have seen many unhappy people here although they might have a lot of money. When you have love in your family, you are never unhappy. In Mexico, you learn that money is not important—love is. You can survive without money, but you cannot be happy without love. Health is also more important than money. Without the body feeling good, you cannot be a happy man.

"If I inherited $100,000 I would go back home and build a new house for my family. We could live comfortably for years. There is no way that would happen, but it is a nice dream, eh?

"If I had enough money I would be free. Now I am not free. I am tied to my job, which I hate. I am forced to work in a little hell. I have dreams of becoming a big star someday, and having a big house with servants. But it is a dream, and nothing more."

THE ELDERLY POOR

The just-me-and-my-hands career is taxing at any age, but especially difficult on men and women as they grow older. The next story points up another category of poor people: the aged and retired. Many people in this category didn't expect to find poverty at the end of their life's journey. They wound up poor for a number of reasons: Some were never in a position financially in the first place to plan for retirement, some planned inadequately due to inflation, and some were caught unaware—especially widows whose husbands died taking financial planning with them into their graves.

Sam is an example of a man who planned but was reduced to a marginal income level anyway:

A retired city worker, Sam is sixty-nine but looks eighty because of his wrinkled, bent body and white hair. Sam feels he's gotten the short end of the Social Security stick. He said: "Money was always the main reason I did the work I did. I wasn't working because I loved the city, or because I enjoyed gardening. I did it for the money and because I could make a good buck out of it here in South San Francisco.

"You've heard of the dirty old man? Well, you might call me the angry old man. I put in forty-two years for the city of San Francisco, and two years after I retired, I'm stuck without enough money to live on. What kind of thanks is that for a job well done?

"I have a wife to support, too, and the only way we've paid our bills the last two years is by me doing gardening jobs on the side for some rich people. I had over forty years of that, but I guess it wasn't enough. I used to be a religious man, but after I got screwed by the city, I turned away from religion. It doesn't do any good to pray for guidance because all you get is problems. I spent forty-two years out in the sun and wind and the cold and the rain, and the thanks I get is a chance to do it all over again for a whole lot less money. I'm working just as hard as I ever did, but I'm only making about half as much.

"I'm not getting any younger, and my body can't take this constant battering. My arthritis is flaring up almost every day, and I have to work in pain. It's a terrible way to live.

"Money does affect me emotionally. I have always tried to stay ahead of the game, and I have never really worried where my next meal is coming from. Even now I have to say that my situation isn't as desperate as most of the people I know who are retired, but that's because I'm willing to hustle for a few bucks while most guys my age are too lazy to do that. But why should I have to work at my age? I have done that all my life."

THE HOMELESS POOR

A new category of homeless people is growing in the United States. These "new poor" owe their existence to basic political and economic changes in American society and their own personal problems, including mental illness, drug and alcohol abuse.

Previous generations of poor, whether the Southern or Eastern European immigrants in the late nineteenth and early twentieth centuries, or the more recent underclass of society formed by minorities, were and are largely ethnic in character and mostly undereducated. The new homeless is a much more mixed group, including unemployed persons, young people whose upward mobility opportunities have been closed off, the mentally ill, substance abusers, and the voluntary poor.

Unemployment and homelessness are the basic characteristics of the new poor. In some parts of the country—such areas of the Midwest previously dominated economically by auto and steel manufacturing—employment prospects seem hopeless for young people. Combined with these unemployment difficulties, recent actions by our government at the federal and state levels have curtailed government funds and involvement in the social and economic needs of people with problems in American society. Unemployment programs have been cut back, funding for social services has been cut, and, increasingly, the burden of dealing with poverty has fallen to local and private charitable organizations. Such efforts have, in many cases, proven to be inadequate, and the number of the homeless has continued to increase.

Joining the homeless population are many de-institutionalized mental patients. While many mental health experts have advocated moving mental patients from large institutions to smaller, community based care programs, funding to do so has in many cases been cut. The result has been that mentally disabled patients, often unable to take care of themselves, are released from institutions with nowhere to go. They quickly join the growing number of homeless in the United States.

Another group of homeless is the voluntary poor, which is an even more mixed group. This group includes people from the 1960's counterculture, who shun traditional American life and are drawn into the simplicity of street life, and very young people, including runaways.

There is no clear definition of the term *homeless*. Under the heading of homeless, various articles talk about such people as drug addicts, alcoholics, teenage runaways, random hippies, poor people, and poor families. According to the U.S. Conference of Mayors (1987), more than one-third of the nation's homeless population consists of families with children—its fastest growing segment. The reason for this is twofold. At the same time as the number of families living below the poverty line has increased because of unemployment and cuts in welfare benefits, the availability of low-cost housing has dropped.

Once a family is homeless, they are likely to encounter discrimination when they seek emergency shelter. In Los Angeles, for example, only 51 of the county's 215 shelters accept families, and of those only 16 accept families with fathers. Though homeless individuals often live outside—on sidewalks and park benches, beneath freeway overpasses—homeless families are more likely to be hidden from the public eye, living marginally from night to night on the streets, in shelters, or in city-provided hotels.

A typical family of this type is the Smith family: Crissy, six; Jesse, four; their twenty-seven-year-old mother, Linda, a former nursing-home aide; and their thirty-three-year-old stepfather, Dean, an ex-trucker. When the Smiths moved to California a month ago, the car transported, housed, and even subsidized them. Before they left their rented trailer outside Colorado Springs, they sold their Skylark's rims, tachometer, and gauges. For nearly two years neither Dean nor Linda had found work in Colorado, a state with a high unemployment rate. They knew that even if they did not find jobs in California, the state's welfare allotments for families were the highest in the nation. They left Colorado on September 6, with eight dollars in cash, and everything they owned stuffed into the trunk. The children bounced up and down, excited by the adventure. The peanut butter and jelly sandwiches ran out by the time they crossed the California border. The money ran out by the time they got to Victorville. Dean panhandled five dollars, which bought enough gas to get to Palmdale, where they sold eight rock tapes for three dollars. They rolled into the San Fernando Valley the night of September 8, with an empty gas tank and less than ten cents.

Dean had been promised a job with a trucking company, but the offer was rescinded because he had no phone number where he could be contacted. "It's a bitch," says Dean. "You can't get a job unless you have a phone. You can't get a phone unless you have an apartment. You can't get an apartment unless you have a job." Regrettably, for homeless poor people, there is a direct negative impact on all family members, especially the children.

Pollster Louis Harris, in his 1987 book, *Inside America,* found that Americans are not oblivious to the lives lived out by the poor and homeless.[1] According to his research:

- ⇨ 67 percent of Americans believe too little effort has been devoted to the problems of the poor.

- ⇨ 73 percent believe the U.S. spends too little effort on the problems of the elderly poor.

- ⇨ 63 percent say too little effort has been directed toward the problems of poor children.

Although these attitudes attest to America's awareness and sensitivity, the government has not responded in proper measure to the severity of the problem.

RELIGION AND MONEY

On a nongovernmental level, many poor Americans have turned to religion as a way of coping with poverty, and for many it can deliver solace, inspiration, and comfort. Unfortunately, they sometimes fall prey to unscrupulous preachers who are more interested in lining their pockets than in helping the poor. As we have seen in the past decade, the Jim Baker approach has bilked the poor, and many people have turned away from televangelism.

An interesting case related to religion and money is the appeal of the Reverend Frederick J. Eichelberger II, a TV evangelist known to millions as the Reverend Ike. He appeals to the poor with a message that is so blatant it seems like a caricature: Salvation is money. His "religion" is actually monetary, playing off the dreams of the poor and confirming their feeling that money is all-important.

The following discussion is derived from a tape of one of Reverend Ike's sermons: "Repeat after me: I have a wonderful relationship with

money . . . money loves me . . . money loves to fill my pockets . . . I
see a mountain of money piling into my arms . . . I see myself on a
shopping spree . . . taking fabulous vacations several times a year—
with money to spare. . . . Oh bless you, money, you're wonderful
stuff."

The Reverend Ike, an unabashed hedonist, a millionaire who flaunts
it in cars, dress, and jewels, preaches that there is healing power,
prospering power, blessing power, and money-drawing power in right
thinking and right giving—giving, that is, to him. His tradition is the
power of positive greed à la Dale Carnegie. And yet, as Ike's cult is
analyzed by religion watchers, it's also noted that he is an important
dispenser of "bootstrap" self-awareness psychology, which can indeed
help the poor escape their poverty.

The son of a South Carolina Baptist preacher, Reverend Ike knew
extreme poverty in his youth, which he is fond of recalling for his
audiences—how he walked barefoot four miles to and from school each
day. His theme, as evidenced in his own personal prescription, is doled
out to his followers in sermons and in *Action* magazine: "Get out of the
ghetto and 'get mo'!"

Using a mix of old-fashioned Bible and classic Horatio Alger, he
advises, "I know what it's about. I used to be black myself . . . then I
went green." He chides, "I know black women can outfry Colonel
Sanders [of the Kentucky Fried Chicken chain] any day . . . so why
ain't you rich? . . . And St. Paul wrote these unfortunate words, 'The
love of money is the root of all evil.' Nobody corrected him until I came
along and had the audacity to say 'The lack of money is the root of all
evil.' " Reverend Ike may have a point on this issue. Poor people are
emotionally battered by a society that provides little help for the
lifestyle most people justifiably seek in American society.

8

Deviance for Dollars

*D*EVIANCE FOR dollars sounds like a new game show, and in a real sense it is a "game" played by a variety of criminals in our society, from the street hood to the white collar criminal. The ordinary criminal does not steal for money alone. When I was director of a community crime prevention program on Manhattan's upper West Side for five years, I carried out a study of over thirty-five cases of muggings, presumably for monetary gain. Muggers followed a typical scenario, which was to hold up a man with a gun or at knife-point, or to snatch a woman's purse and run. Initially, this scene appears to be a robber using violence to get money from a victim.

Upon closer investigation, in over fifteen cases I found that the acting out of the violence against the victim was more important to the mugger than the money. Often a person commits a delinquent act out of some emotional disorder. In such cases, taking the money serves as a "rational" cloak of immunity to the violent act. It's the violence that is the payoff for some pathological criminals, not just the money. In many of these mugging cases, the offender often had a docile, willing victim, a "take my money and leave me alone" person, so he had to inflame the situation in order to give himself the rationale for violence. Getting his money wasn't enough, or wasn't totally what he was after.

In one particular case, the modus operandi of a purse-snatcher involved selecting an older woman, beating her unmercifully, and then, almost as an afterthought, taking her money. In an intensive interview I conducted with this nineteen-year-old youth, there was some evidence that he was fulfilling an emotional need to inflict assaults on women resembling his own mother. He had a strict oppressive mother and was compulsively beating up older female victims with his displaced aggression.

A more basic connection between crime and money is found in the deprived lower classes rebelling and fighting back against an oppressive society. William A. Bonger, a Dutch sociologist, applies a Marxist explanation to crime and delinquency, and blames the capitalist system. In Bonger's view, people have two potential sides: altruistic and selfish. Capitalism stimulates the selfish side. People produce for profit. Intense competition is the norm, between employers, who try to exploit workers for the lowest wages, and laborers who try to sell their work for the highest monetary price.

In this selfish, egotistic competition, business people sink to becoming parasites, regarding workers as objects to make profits, and feeling no moral obligation toward them. This unfair, unbalanced, unplanned system frequently breaks down because factories overproduce and close, because underpaid workers underconsume goods they can't afford. The results of capitalism, according to Bonger, are unemployment, increased poverty, greater inequality, and greater resentment—all adding up to crime, another expression of human selfishness. In his words, the working classes retaliate with crimes of vengeance against those who exploit them.[1]

Bonger is a radical, but he is not alone in analyzing crime and concluding that the payoff is vengeance and social rebellion. Albert K. Cohen, a sociologist, also defined delinquency as a form of revolt against the middle class values rather than merely an act to get money. He calls the delinquent subculture "non-utilitarian, malicious, and negativistic."[2]

Stealing "for the hell of it" delivers profit and more—glory, prowess, and satisfaction are crime payoffs, too. There is no rational way to explain the effort, danger, and risk involved in stealing items which are often later discarded, destroyed, or given away casually. Delinquents are often poor and do steal things that are valued, but much stealing— clothes they will never wear or objects they will never use—is done in retaliation, with vengeance as crucial a motive as economics.

Another feature of the criminal mind is its opportunistic nature. According to David Matz, many psychopathic offenders can't pass up a good scam, and so they "drift" into delinquency.[3] I put this theory to the test as I interviewed twenty criminals, all of whom had spent time in prison.

We discussed the relative merits of obtaining money legally versus illegally. Most of them were legally working as part of rehabilitation programs. However, fierce arguments erupted because many felt turning down a good "hustle" would still be foolish. The group smiled when I pointed out most people *never* thought about illegally supplementing their income. In fact, they seemed shocked when I told them they were unique because they saw illegal means of getting money as an ever-present possibility, alongside honest work.

Several of the criminals in the group objected to this statement, pointing out that white collar criminals, like politicians, indulge in upper-class thievery. I had to agree that people in any stratum can drift into criminal opportunities when the opportunity arises.

Dr. John Irwin is one of the most perceptive observers of the crime scene in America. His understanding stems from unique credentials: He's a one-time convicted armed robber, originator of the drive-in robbery in California, for which he spent five years in Soledad Prison. After prison, he went straight, graduated from UCLA, and went on to get a Ph.D. in sociology from UC Berkeley. John is now a renowned criminologist and professor of sociology at San Francisco State University. One of his important books was *The Felon*. His twofold perspective as both a former criminal and criminologist reveals many penetrating insights into the emotional meaning of money to a criminal.

"I didn't get into deviant ways of making money until I was fifteen. I wanted extra commodities, not so much money. Money itself was never a big thing to me, but I did have a strong desire for things, as most kids do. I got caught stealing rocket ships out of a dimestore at six. I got caught stealing playing cards. The neighborhood kids were into collecting playing cards. I really got serious about stealing when I was about fifteen or sixteen and I became interested in Roadsters. Owning a Roadster was it. A Roadster is a particular creation of LA, a Model A usually or sometimes Model T which has been remodified with a V-8 motor. It had special wheels, no fenders, and other special things. There were certain types of Roadsters that all the guys were trying to get; and for us it was quite an expensive hobby.

"I worked for a time in a bowling alley, setting pins for about $30 a week. I was sticking every cent into an old Roadster body. I still had $500 of work left to do, including elaborate upholstery. I got into some heavy stealing to raise the money. A Roadster brought respect and success and girls in my little high school world.

"At around seventeen I'd been through that car phase and I had kind of grown out of it. At that time I started hanging around in another social world. I began hanging around a pool hall with a selected group of friends who were much more into criminal hoodlum activities. They were boozing a lot, smoking marijuana and partying. A lot of them were into pool hustling and stealing. Being tough was a very important part of the scene. A lot of guys there were successful amateur and almost professional fighters in this little town of San Fernando. San Fernando had a tough working class group, half Mexican, half white, Italian, and others. We started stealing heavily at about eighteen. When the opportunity arose, we stole. We would yank telephones, any money we could get our hands on. Sometimes with a crowbar we would hit fifteen phone boxes and wind up with $100 or so.

"About this time I came into more contact with professional thieves. For them a very important value was the big score. I was starting to absorb some of their values. The big score is a large hunk of money acquired through one good caper. A good caper would be a safe or armed robbery. We wanted the money. We didn't like the experience. We were scared to death. The goal was getting through it, the relief of having made it and getting the money. Maybe there were thieves that got a hard-on from the experience, but that wasn't our bunch. Our bunch would have rather had somebody else go do it and hand us the money. Believe it, it was the money. And the money was used to live a lifestyle which we had learned to like. The lifestyle involved having a nice car, good clothes, leisure, and hanging around all day with money in your pocket, and getting broads more easily. We didn't want to work for our money. Money gave us a freedom from work and joining what we saw as a rotten, square society.

"I scraped through high school and they didn't want to give me my diploma because I got straight D's in my last year. In '47, they were converting some factories around LA to commercial airlines. I went over and worked one week for one of them. I hated it and never showed up again. I'm reminded of the movie *A Thousand Clowns,* when Jason Robards shows his nephew people going to work every morning and says, 'I want to show you something really ugly; people going to work.' And it was really ugly to me.

"About this time my gang was really getting into big money. We were being indoctrinated into a criminal subculture. The notion of honesty with each other in our group was so strong it was scary. If you found out a guy bullshitted you, you never rapped with him again. So we were not just dog-eat-dog—that ideology was repulsive to us. Some of us learned a very sophisticated rationale for our thievery. There was a book, *The Rebellion of Leo McGuire,* about a thief with a sophisticated socialistic rationale for his theft. We were influenced by the ideas in the book.

"Our attitude toward the upper classes was that they deserved to be stolen from. They were exploiters. It was all right to take their money. There was a more pragmatic reason—it's easier to steal from people who are insured. They put up less of a squawk. If you steal from the little guys, they're liable to pull a gun out and shoot you to hang onto their money.

"In the thieves' culture, the ideal is that you caper as infrequently as possible. One a year, because you don't want to be a working class slob, a cheating capitalist pig, just to live in this lousy arrangement the best you can. The Brinks million dollar caper was the prototype we admired.

"I became involved in taking off safes. My group and I started getting bigger scores. We'd look over telephone companies, P.G. & E. One night we burned a safe open in a telephone company—$1800 for four hours' work. I went out and bought a car, clothes, with a nice little sneer on my face to indicate I was doing okay.

"In those days we were constantly looking for money. We'd spend almost every day looking for a good caper. Around then I initiated the drive-in robbery. I noticed a lot of gas stations had a check-cashing window, a big service, a lot of money.

"There's no thrill involved, things are too tense. Your tongue is thick, sometimes you can't even talk. Once you're away and have the money, there's another emotion—happiness. You smile ear to ear. You got away with it. You got some money to last you for a while. Each caper lifts you for a while out of that feeling of despondency that comes from being broke.

"My last caper before Soledad was armed robbery involving one of these gas stations. I had heard that this place had five grand. So there I was waving this gun in the face of the woman behind the counter. She gave me $900. Later on I checked with the guy who had told me about the $5000. He found out where they kept the rest of the money. Joking, I said, 'Those bastards owe me four grand, let's go back and get it.'

"By that time we'd done five or six of these capers and the local police were getting pissed off. The Burbank police were out to get us. They had a stake-out, but we pulled in fifteen minutes after the stake-out left. But the owner had a gun. My partner went in, the owner comes out shooting. He was a lousy shot. He was so nervous he didn't hit anything. Jim fires one shot to get him out of the doorway. Jim makes it out and into the car. We both had loaded guns and a good shot at the guy, but neither of us wanted to possibly kill the guy. We hauled ass in our car and got away. We dumped the stolen car, but Jim left his jacket in it, stupidly. They tracked us down. We each got five years to life at Soledad.

"The five years I spent in prison were, in one way, valuable in giving me much of the data I later used in my Ph.D. dissertation and my book The Felon.

"What is the meaning of money to criminals? The inequities and the hollowness of chasing money dreams tends to gain a little less strength in prison. People begin to think of nonmoney pursuits, try to figure another way to live. To some extent they look back at their criminal attempts as the failures they were.

"Most prisoners are poor slobs in and out of prison. Prisons are full of poor people. Even the successful thieves who talk about the big scores, they're lying. Nobody really made any big scores. I was one of the most successful with a $4000 caper. Only a few got bigger scores. The successful score is a rare, rare thing. There's only been a few in the history of the country. There are not very many rich criminals. Most of the people are down-and-outers, trying to explore ways of giving up crime, settling down, and taking on a working class lifestyle. Getting a good old lady was probably the most talked-about future lifestyle.

"Well, I've done pretty well since those days. I didn't go into business, I went into academia. As a professor and chair of the department at San Francisco State University, I make enough money to get by, and have some prestige in my community. My monetary needs are not exorbitant. Money as a status symbol means nothing to me. As far as status and power go, I hope the people who count to me like my books. I've written in sociology. If I made $100,000 out of a book, great! But if I had my choice between money and the acceptance, I'd still prefer the acceptance of my colleagues.

"No, there is no amount of money that would seduce me back into crime, not even a million dollars. But frankly, I have more respect for a guy who pulls a big caper than these punks who become folk heroes like the Beatles, who are showered with money for no reason. Most criminals are driven by circumstances to earn money by crime. I now respect people who really contribute to society."

"Dr. Irwin's story illustrates the life of most lower class criminals. This contrasts with the subject of my next interview, Albie Baker, who was a professional thief. Most professional criminals abhor violence, are masters at craft and profit. Albie stole jewels for money and status. When I interviewed him, he was sixty and no longer a criminal—he was earning a reasonable living as a screenwriter.

"My whole drive toward money is related to the diamond as more of a symbol than anything, a symbol of money and power. I wasn't driven to money for the sake of money. I passed the point of achieving the amounts of money I felt necessary. The most money I ever had in cash was around $170,000. I paid for my ill-gotten gains in many ways, spending over twelve years in various prisons.

"There was a bigger penalty. Money destroyed me. It destroyed a great talent I had. I now know since I used my skills as a writer that the money I made as a jewel thief cut my motivation to write and wasted all those years. [Albie Baker wrote *Stolen Sweets,* an excellent autobiography about his life as a jewel thief.]

"My first recollection of my father was that he was incapable of earning money. When I was thirteen I could go out and make more money out of petty crime in one day than he would make in an entire week. I simply went out and stole. When I was a bit older, I had a kind of crazy theory that money provided a partial freedom for a more expanded vision of life. The freedom I obtained through money got me out of a poor home in Brooklyn.

"My first big score? Oh, that's very vivid. That's like it was yesterday. Well, I had been stealing on a certain level, that say earned me $400 to $1000 a week. I had to work as a thief almost every day, and at least one or two days a week physically commit a crime. I must have been about eighteen or nineteen, and I decided to change my environment—my stealing environment, my modus operandi, my whole conceptual approach. Don't forget, we, especially in the United States, are a movie culture and we reflect what we see in film—not literature or books so much as film. And like every other American kid, I was a victim of the movies. I wanted to live the kind of life that I saw in films. When I was twelve I saw a movie called *Grand Hotel* and it made such an impression on me that I began to act it out at nineteen.

"It was one of the first great all-star films. Every star of that era was in it, John Barrymore, Wallace Beery, and Greta Garbo. The character I remember most was John Barrymore. He was very elegant, dressed in tails and a top hat. He drank champagne and was surrounded by beauties in this very elegant hotel, but he was desperate for money. Only the audience knew this because everything else about him was a front. And one day he goes up to the Grand Hotel and he goes out of his window, and he's crawling along the edge and enters into a bedroom. He's in the process of stealing the jewels when this beautiful woman comes in. It's Greta Garbo—and he's all embarrassed. . . . I forgot how he got out of there. I only remember the type of person he was, living the kind of life he was, and yet he was a thief. And I said to myself, if I'm going to be a crook, I'm going to be that kind of a crook. The John Barrymore suave, elegant type of criminal fit my image of what I wanted to become.

"I never wanted to be a Humphrey Bogart, Jimmy Cagney, or George Raft, because I was never violence-prone. I didn't believe in weapons or guns or anything like that. And I didn't believe in head-on-confrontation crime. I wanted to become a *Grand Hotel* thief like John Barrymore, and that's what I did most of my life as a jewel thief.

"Connected to my decision was the fact that I was an avid reader besides going to the movies. I read all of the great novels and the popular novels of the day and magazines and newspapers. It didn't take much imagination to realize that the kind of people who had the kind of jewelry and money I wanted did not live in poor neighborhoods like I did, the Bronx or Brooklyn. My father didn't know any, my mother didn't know any of these people, and I didn't know any of them. So I bought a car and I started to drive.

"I got a map of the suburbs of New York and I read in the newspapers about Meadowbrook in Long Island, where they would have the polo games; Sands Point, where they had all the big estates; Greenwich, Connecticut, where all the stockbrokers lived. And I got to know those areas better than I knew the streets of the Bronx. I got to understand how the police worked, what kind of cars they used and the habits of these rich people. And it wasn't long before I settled on a section of Greenwich, Connecticut, called Rockhill. I think it's the oldest part of Greenwich. They're all like English colonial houses or Tudor homes. I also developed the instinct of knowing when nobody was at home. The first house I hit had an enormous greenhouse full of flowers. I just drove up the driveway and, actually through stupidity and not knowing my business, I did everything wrong—but the end result was right. I just drove up, knocked on the door, and in case anyone were to answer, I would ask for some fictitious name or direction. No one answered the door and I kept ringing. No one answered. And I walked around to the back of the house, to the back service door, rang that bell. There was nobody home. I broke in and ran through the house. It took no training as a burglar to know that if you're going to find anything, it's probably going to be in the master bedroom.

"That was my first big score—the master bedroom. Sitting right up on a chest of drawers was an enormous jewel box, jammed with jewels. At this point, I didn't even know where to sell the stuff. I got back to the old neighborhood, saw a couple of old thieves, and they gave me $12,000. My feeling then was that I had all the money in the world.

"How did it affect my life? In one sense it ruined me because I was so spoiled with money. I thought there was an endless supply. In between these capers I got arrested, served some prison sentences, came out, continued again. I felt very free, as opposed to friends I knew, who were locked into problems, early marriages, children at an early age, jobs they despised. I felt lucky because they were in prison just as sure as I had been. The only thing is that in between prison terms I had great rewards.

"Money enlarged my circle of friends. I lived in the best hotels. I kept a suite. I gave parties. I entertained. I was always as beautifully dressed as they were. I had the best cars. I was known by all the people who owned the best restaurants. I acted just like the rich. I watched the way they acted. I took on their affectations, their mannerisms. I did all the things that these people did.

"In those days my life had no middle ground. I had money or I was locked up and dreamed about it. I dreamed about the money and the life I was going to have when I got out. There was no thought of reformation, none of that jazz.

"I had no guilt about what I did to the wealthy. I don't have any feelings like that when I'm working. I'm working so fast, at such a high level of intensity, that I don't get into thought processes other than to get the jewelry and get out. Diamonds to me had as much significance as the bone in a Swahilis nose. Even a Goselin tapestry or a Louis IV chair to me was worthless. I hated all of the jewelry. All I wanted was the money and the lifestyle it brought me.

"One thing that gratified me a lot and was a big motivation in my life was women. I might add that I was extremely successful with them. One day I met a beautiful model. At a dinner party, we broke away and went off by ourselves. We always sensed an attraction toward each other, I had known her in New York. She knew all about my past. What she didn't know was that I had to appear in Santa Monica court at 8:00 A.M. the next morning. We got home and had our big sexual affair and we stayed up. In the morning I had some juice and coffee, took a taxi to the courtroom, and was sentenced to two years in jail. For those two years I thought, 'Well at least I had a good send-off. I'd balled this beautiful girl.'

"My peak experience was a score I took in this house in upper New York State in a wealthy area. I was just driving around when, as chance would have it, I saw a Cadillac, a very well-dressed man and woman getting into the car. I watched them leave their palatial home. I followed them onto the highway for about five miles, and passed them. I headed back to their house. They had all the night lights set up. I broke in. The bedroom was dark. I had no flashlight, so I took matches and lit them. The bedroom closet had a double lock. I opened it and there was a metal strongbox, not a safe. I opened it and in there were packages of jewels and a bunch of envelopes. I jammed them into my pockets without counting the currency in them. I got home and started to count the money. There was around $170,000 cash in the envelopes! The money was dirty, either black market or from some other illegal source.

"Later in life it wasn't just the money I wanted anymore. I even got to despise money because I saw the corruption it did to my own family and friends. I was kind of burned out with all that kind of life. Getting up one morning I decided I was flying to Paris first class. I would rent a house in St. Tropez for the winter, stay a month and get bored. But I can't totally put down my past life. I did get to meet Cocteau, Picasso, Genet, and other people like them.

"My interests changed completely. I wanted something more and found it, in part, as a writer. I was interested in people who had a talent. They were smart, intelligent, and that I could relate to.

"In retrospect, I have regrets. If I had stopped stealing and continued my education, I might have become a more successful writer. I no longer desire the kind of money I had. I wouldn't want to be a big man in that sense, do any of the things I had previously done with money. I would want to be recognized for the output that would come out of my consciousness, which would be writing."

Albie Baker may have hobnobbed with the upper class society, but the modus operandi of his crime—burglary—was essentially "lower class." "Upper class" thievery uses different methods. As Jim a twenty-three-year old con convicted for check fraud, said, "You show me a businessman who isn't a crook in some part of his work. And the politicians are worse than they are. They all get plenty of graft. I'm a small-time operator by comparison. But I write a lousy bad check for $100 and I'm locked up. Boesky and Milken steal billions and get off easy. I write a bad check and go to prison. Is that fair?"

No, it's not fair; it's white collar crime. Perhaps Jim overstates the case a bit, but business and government are rife with cases to support his frustrations. In the last two decades, public service has become almost a masquerade for profiteers. From the Robert Vesco and ITT scandals implicating the Nixon administration, to the influence peddlers and Pentagon scandal of the Reagan Cabinet, government officials in far too many cases have crossed the criminal boundaries. Big business readily conspires in illicit takeovers, and billions of dollars are stolen by savings and loan executives in the normal course of their business. Wall Street rocked in the 80s with Ivan Boesky and insider trading scams, and the 90s promise more as Boesky cooperates with federal officials.

In these contexts, the machinations of professional white collar, political, and organized crime criminals involve enormous amounts of money. Principles are readily for sale. The actors in these dramas are generally psychopathic insatiables with limited or no social conscience, and certainly no remorse. They abuse their positions of trust strictly for the dollars and the power they can obtain in the process. Crime pays on all levels, with payoffs as varied as the criminals.

PROSTITUTION AND DOLLARS

Most simply stated, prostitution is the exchange of sex for money. However, it becomes more complicated than that. There are essentially three players—the prostitute, the customer (known as "the John"), and in some, but not all cases, the pimp, agent, or madam. In the case of a recent Washington, D.C. prostitution ring, the madam was a mister.

The reasons given by prostitutes for entering the oldest profession have often been discounted. It appears to me that their insights about their own occupational choice are as important to consider as any. In one study 90 percent of the prostitutes listed money as their prime motivation. Two thirds said they had "no regrets."

Opal, twenty-five, came to Las Vegas to become a show girl and wound up a prostitute, an independent one, without a pimp. "I have no regrets for anything that's happened to me or that I've done. I've had a chance to sleep with some of the top men in the show business world, and I've made more money turning tricks than I ever could have any other way back in Pennsylvania. The reason I went into this business was because money is more important to me than anything else. I have done the work only because of the money, although in most cases it has been very pleasant for me. I don't have any complaints about the way I've been treated here.

"I didn't really have a father. He was gone before I ever met him. I was raised by my mother in Pittsburgh, and she did everything to keep me on the straight and narrow, but I was a rebellious child. I came out to Vegas six years ago. I completely forgot everything she told me about money. I just wanted to make as much as I could as fast as I could. I have saved very little. I find myself with so many incidental expenses all the time and no way to pay them except through hustling. I have a beautiful apartment and a new Jag.

"I try not to spend my money gambling. It is really one of the only rules I have. While everybody else is going nuts trying to throw all the money they make down the sewer, I have decided I'm not going to throw money away.

"I steal when I can. If a trick is stupid enough to leave his wallet and money when he goes to the john, it won't be there when he gets back. Oh I've had plenty of creepy pimps try to take me over, but why should I give them money? It's ridiculous. I'm strictly out for me."

The pimp issue raised by Opal is complicated. In a discussion I had with several ex-addicts and ex-pimps, one bright young man cited interesting social historical roots from the days of slavery, when black women in bondage were forced to have sexual relationships with white men, slave owners and oppressors. After being sexually humiliated, many a slave would be given money, trinkets, clothes, or extra food. She would take her "payments" back to her black lover, who would soothe her bad feelings over the incident, share in these spoils, and together they would ridicule the white oppressor. Whether or not this analysis is sound, it does raise an interesting question.

According to Harold Greenwald in his classic study, *The Call Girl,* prostitutes turn their money over to pimps to overcome loneliness and form a relationship with someone. Prostitutes have a history of parental deprivation in early childhood. Their occupation becomes a vehicle in which they search for someone to take care of them, to care for them in a way they missed out on originally. The money they receive is a symbol of warmth, love, even value. As one prostitute said, "Money from a trick gives me some value. My family always looked at me as a nobody of no value. But every day I meet men who want me enough to give me money." It is understandable that the slang word for money is often "bread." In other words, prostitutes do not turn tricks and turn over the money to their agent-pimps for bread alone.

A former pimp described it this way: "Along comes this guy they've already heard about: Joe Pimp. And he gives 'em a little attention. Hangin' out with Joe Pimp is better than loneliness, and don't forget, they're broke. They don't know how to earn any money. They get sucked up into the lifestyle with Joe Pimp and some little group of girls. A lot of these pimp families are gathered and controlled by women. She's encouraged to become part of Joe Pimp's enterprise, which is more successful, will put some order in her life, and earn her some money. She doesn't even think of the money as hers or his, it's theirs. He's giving her something for her money. With Joe Pimp she joins a family. They have an apartment with three or four girls. They get friendly. The pimp family becomes important."

Another feature identified in Greenwald's study is hostility toward men. Greenwald notes that prostitutes often have been abused by an older man in their early years. Prostitution is a way of striking back at men, humiliating them and taking their money in the process.

One example is Jane, a beautiful twenty-five year old actress who when not succeeding in film becomes a waitress, hat check girl, and finally a call girl. Her anger is obvious. "You sell your body because it's the last thing you have to sell. It feels really good to fuck over men, because they've fucked me and fucked me over for many years. As a hooker for $200 or more, I'm in charge of them instead of the opposite.

"As an aspiring actress I've taken their shit for many years. I remember the first time I had a shot for a part. This producer began to tell me all of the things he was going to do for me. He had this plush office. Suddenly he begins to slobber all over me. He locked the door and he started to rape me on this leather sofa. When I began to scream, he stopped. Then he threw me out of his office.

"These last few years were all depressing from the standpoint of money. I never had anything extra, just enough to scrape by. I was stuck, the most depressing thing was it seemed there was no way out. Every week I'd have to scrimp for food, or go out with a creep to be fed. I got tired of standing in unemployment lines. I found that more degrading than what I do now.

"My parents never had any money, but they always managed to put food on my plate and give me a warm place to sleep. They used to teach me to save my pennies, but that's been useless out here, because until recently I never had anything to save. I always used to find guys who were down and out for some reason. I guess I felt more at ease with guys who were broke like I was. But now the worm has turned.

"Fuck those guys. And screw all of those Mickey Mouse waitress and other bullshit jobs I took to keep trying here. I'll never go back to that again. Now I'm in charge. These assholes come to my place. They're all pretty rich or they couldn't afford me. I get $200 an hour. Some of them come in three seconds flat and I nicely kick their asses right out of my door.

"I've only been at it for a year, but I love it. Some of these big pricks are into bondage. They want to crawl, kiss your feet, have you piss on them. I can't bring myself to do that yet, but believe me, it's very trendy here in Hollywood. One of the biggest stars in this town—he's a comic—goes for that. I won't tell you his name because that goes against my code.

"Why do they like to be dominated? I'm no psychologist, but I think they feel guilty about all the money and power they have. So they relieve some of this guilt by getting a working girl to literally shit on them, and then they pay her for it.

"As an aspiring actress, I've taken their abuse for many years. I've been in Hollywood seven years now, trying to make it. I've had a few walk-on parts. It's a big pain, though. I've just about had it with producers in this town. I promised myself that if I didn't get a break by the time I was twenty-five, I would get out. But it's not easy to give up. I don't want to give up, and that's why I'm still plugging. And now that I don't have to constantly worry about money because of what I earn hustling, I can pursue my career better."

Another prostitute, Madeline, thirty-one, takes issue with psychological theories about her work as a prostitute. Although she is lower down on the hooker ladder, she simply feels the money is good.

"You can't shit me, man. You want to paint the picture of a poor little girl who was neglected and had to turn her back on society, but in this case it just ain't so.

"I could have been a lot of things, but I decided to go out on the street to make a lot of money doing something I liked that I was good at. You can't ask for much more than that from any job. I really did enjoy it for about a year. Now it's a job, just like any other. It's like working the graveyard shift at a plant, except the working conditions are a little better and the pay is a whole lot better.

"Money is the only reason I stay on the street. Money is where it's at, and I'll do anything and everything with anyone for the right amount of cash. If that doesn't say it all, nothing does. The money turns over real fast. On a good night I can make $1000. Nothing else can touch that.

"There is nothing more important to me than money. I have a lot of pride in myself because I know I have made it out of the ghetto. I live in Los Feliz and lounge around all day long. I don't usually get up till about three and then I'm out on the street by nine. The excitement keeps me going. Always on the move, meeting new people. All kinds of people. Not any one kind, but a potluck group. I really enjoy it.

"I've got no complaints. I didn't get a lot of help from my parents. My daddy left home when I was five and my momma was on relief. We didn't give a shit about anything and I never bothered to learn a thing in school because nothing really mattered. I knew by the time I made it into high school that I was going to make it on the streets."

In prostitution, the money factor is important in another way. In almost all professions, one must first gain experience and knowledge, and then over the years hope to see an increase in volume. With prostitution the opposite occurs most often. Very big money is earned soon after starting. Novelty is highly marketable, giving a novice the advantage over more experienced and better known competitors on the street, even though they may be more sexually experienced and smoother at interpersonal techniques. The new girl, looks and personal qualities aside, has considerable drawing power because she provides a new sexual experience to the customer. Early success and financial reward may well provide considerable incentive for a woman to continue in the occupation.

GAMBLERS—GETTING INTO THE
ACTION

Gambling is an American institution, a great American pastime. Almost two out of three Americans place some kind of bet each year. According to one survey, over 80 percent of the public gambles. Fifteen and a half million Americans gamble legally. Eighty-eight million participate in some form. The revenue from gambling was estimated to be well over $200 billion a year in 1989, and gambling of all kinds is on the rise.[4]

Why do people gamble? Reasons cited most often include "to have a good time," "to pass the time," "to be challenged," and "to make money." For people who gamble legally, the fear of arrest is the biggest reason they don't make illegal bets. For legal bettors, the fear of losing money doesn't seem to matter. However, two-thirds of nonbettors listed "fear of losing money" as one of their biggest deterrents. Also, almost half of nonbettors say they don't gamble because gambling is immoral.

It is estimated that there are well over a million compulsive gamblers in the United States. One study reveals that gambling is related to marital problems, crime, job dissatisfaction, and other addictions like alcohol and substance abuse. Compulsive gamblers are driven to bizarre atrocious behaviors to get their "action money" or stake.

One man I interviewed related this example. His mother had died suddenly on a Friday morning. Asked by his sister to contribute toward the funeral, Barry said he was broke. That afternoon, he went to the Aqueduct racetrack and blew $200 on the horses. Barry says, "That money was action money and to a compulsive gambler like me, that meant it was strictly for gambling, nothing else, not even my own mother's funeral."

Charlie recalls the night his wife discovered her bracelet missing. Aware of her husband's gambling, she asked him if he had taken the bracelet. Indignant, he denied taking it and proceeded to turn the house upside down. Charlie recollects, "I even sifted through the garbage looking for it and convinced her I hadn't taken it. Finally, I told her I thought her son by a previous marriage, who had been over the night before, had taken it. She broke down and cried like a baby."

All the while, Charlie knew where the bracelet was—at a pawn shop where he had left it that morning to get some action money for the track that day.

Tony B. was hardly a model father, having looted his daughter's piggybank on numerous occasions, cashed in his son's bonds, and stolen much of his wife's jewelry. But even he knew he'd gone too far when, the day before his daughter's wedding, he withdrew the wedding money to pay off some of the interest he owed to a loan shark.

All of these men share an addiction and are members of Gamblers Anonymous, a self-help group founded by two ex-complusive gamblers in 1957. Gamblers Anonymous, in 1990, has over 20,000 members, 300 national chapters, and 450 chapters worldwide. GA's theory is "it takes one to know one," and "it takes one to help one." Members come from all walks of life and from virtually every financial stratum. There are no dues. The only requirement is a sincere desire to stop gambling.

At a recent meeting which is in essence mass therapy where one recounts gambling horror stories in an effort to overcome his own addiction and help others in their struggle, Harry D. related how he'd sold his blood for gambling money. Al C.'s wife gave birth to a seven-pound, four-ounce girl. With the ten cents she gave him to phone relatives with the good news, he said, "I was completely tapped out and I used the dime to call my bookmaker to place a daily double bet on the seven and four combinations and the four and seven combinations. I won, but I still owed the shylocks $10,000."

Lou M., while a garment company accountant, swindled the firm out of several thousand dollars but never got caught. Subsequently, he served two years in prison for a robbery he staged to help pay off a loan shark who had threatened him with violence.

Why does one become a compulsive gambler? One theory is that gambling is a form of masochism and self-flagellation. Many compulsive gamblers come from broken homes. Most had domineering mothers who showed little affection for them. They are trying to buy love, a substitute kind of love in the form of money. Many psychiatrists and psychologists believe obsessive gamblers have a subconscious desire to lose, not win.

This self-destructive bent is, of course, not true of all gamblers. The "hustler" is another category of gambler. He always wins, because he is a cheater who uses crooked cards, dice, or techniques. Ed, who was a hustler in his teenage years, matured out of the "business" and is now a successful psychologist. Here, he looks back at his hustling days as a youth.

"From the ages of fifteen to twenty-five, I was a hustling gambler. Basically, I cheated people out of their money by 'gambling' with cards and dice. I never lost because I knew how to manipulate the cards and dice to my advantage.

"Focusing on money and gambling, the first thing I would say was winning money was always a fantastic emotional experience. When I beat someone, I loved the feel and the texture of money, and the things I could buy. I felt superior to all the squares who got money either from their parents or from working.

"Money and marks [victims] are interesting. I am absolutely convinced there are sucker gamblers who want you to take their money. When I was sixteen, I had a ritual with this mark. It was almost like a whore and a trick. On Friday, this guy and I would meet at a bowling alley. After our first dice game, from then on, without speaking a word, he and I would shoot dice alone, head to head, in the alley in back of the bowling establishment. I would always win because I used crooked dice. There must have been a pathology and a desire to give up a week's salary when a guy does this fifteen weeks in a row. He must have known I cheated him, and yet there was never a complaint of any kind. After the tenth time, I thought of saying, 'You know you can't win, look at these dice. Why don't you just give your week's pay and save us the time from this boring ritual?' I, of course, never did because he, of course, received some masochistic pleasure from losing his money.

"My conclusions about my early years as a dice hustler are that money was a medium around which we all acquired some gratification. The mark I described was a masochist. The money was a means for satisfying various kinds of emotional needs we all had."

In my research, I administered my questionnaire to several members of Gamblers Anonymous. In summary, it revealed that money, as an end in itself, was more important to men gamblers than to women gamblers. Men spoke of money in more emotional terms. There was a disproportionate number of Insatiables among male gamblers, and their gambling was, in part, an effort to get rich quick. Wives indicated their gambling husbands didn't see the effects their behavior had in their lives and relationships. For example, gamblers were seldom home to carry on a good relationship. Sex lives were affected, too. As one said, "Who wants to make love to a lying, gambling husband who loves the race track more than his family?"

From the gambling man's point of view, one man admitted, "I once balled my wife strictly to get action money out of her. Then I split for the track. It's hard to be sexy when you're broke." Another said, "I'd rather gamble than have sex."

Almost all of the gambler respondents attributed emotional highs or lows to gambling experiences. "My best emotional experience was winning $1500 on a $5 bet; my lowest, every time I lost." Almost all revealed that they "constantly" fought with their spouses over money. Ninety percent felt "foolish" in handling money when gambling and "sensible" when not gambling. Many also noted they felt *insatiable* when gambling and more *logical* and *contented* when not. The majority of compulsive gamblers always lost in the end because no matter how much money they won, they wanted more. This statement epitomizes their syndrome: "I was like an alky with a need for booze. I wanted to win every chip in that casino and break the bank. Of course, I never knew when to quit and almost always lost in the end."

Many gamblers now free from their addiction had fears about this question: What would you do if you inherited $5 million? They feared they'd return to gambling.

Money is the dazzling prize that attracts millions to gambling. The emotional process of gambling involves the opportunity for a quick, simple, direct way to acquire money—or to dispose of it quickly. For people who venerate money and are self-destructive, gambling provides the masochistic condition—destruction—they seek. I've observed that people seem to want to gamble more at certain points in their lives. Gambling can deliver euphoria, an emotional high as money opens up new horizons. Winning money can cure depression, at least temporarily. Without money at its root, betting would be meaningless. In gambling, money's where the action is. Money is what prompts people to get into the action.

Sports gambling is a fascinating aspect of the problem. The case of the legendary Pete Rose, gambling on baseball, is an enigma because of his denial, despite overwhelming evidence, that he bet on the sport. I would speculate, however, that for "Charley Hustle," especially when he became a manager, his motivation for danger pushed him into the self-destructive activity of gambling. Money, in Pete Rose's case, appeared to be a secondary factor to his quest for excitement.

DRUGS ARE DOLLARS

In the drug world, drugs are dollars and dollars are drugs, inter-changeable commodities in terms of value. As in gambling, there are dealers and suckers. From one perspective, though, all participants in the drug drama—from the biggest dealer on down to the lowest strung-out street junkie—are victims. Money has a peculiar, intrinsic position in the machinations that surround the sale and the use of drugs.

A crack cocaine dealer I interviewed had these comments on his "work" and its relationship to money: "What would I do if I got a $100,000 free and clear? Half of it would go in the bank, and the other half I'd deal with. I would buy kilos of gold bud and red bud Columbian, bricks of commercial, and a half pound of cocaine. I'd sell enough to make triple my profit and keep the rest. . . . I'd give people good deals 'cause I'd be getting good deals. I would provide a community service of dope, at low prices. I'd buy a beautiful place and fly my own plane to make deliveries of dope. I'd also invest in stocks and buy view lots at the beach. It makes you feel pretty good. You need money to survive in this world. If you don't have it, forget it; you can't exist without it, you need it. Especially if you have something you want to do. I can't exist without money and dope. It buys enjoyment and relaxation. Life right now is getting stoned on drugs and money.

"I've ripped off my friends many times because of money. I've gotten bad dope deals and I've given bad deals. When I get bad deals, I then fuck over someone else. That's the way the business is, man.

"A depressing experience with money? One is when I see nice Columbian grass that I wish I could have but can't afford it. Right now I can afford it, fortunately. Is it worth it? Yes, it's worth it—many times I wonder, but just as long as you're having fun or a good time in your work, it's good. I feel close to being financially stable, maybe a couple more deals, then I will be. I started dealing about a year ago. Then I got into it heavily. What made me want to start dealing? To meet a lot of strange people. It's fun, something to do that is profitable. You can enjoy yourself and work at the same time.

"I love the way I earn my living. I get stoned regularly and provide a valuable service for people. Whatever money I make I plow right back into the business."

CRACK AND CASH

There are, to be sure, complex social-psychological issues related to the monstrous problems of substance abuse. However, the drug wars of the 1990s, which costs in the billions, essentially revolves around the social problems of poverty, violence, and money.

In an incisive *New York Times* article (August 2, 1988) on crack cocaine and money, Peter Kerr presents some relevant cases that reveal the relationship between the emotional issues of money as they relate to dealing drugs:

> A life inside the drug trade is often solitary, brutal, and short. But to many poor or working-class New Yorkers—victims of a decline of the blue-collar industries that once offered high-paying jobs to people without college degrees—the rewards of the drug business now seem so great, and the risks of punishment so slight, that entering the trade is a powerful lure.
>
> The multibillion-dollar drug business, in fact, is one of the city's largest employers. And those who engage in the traffic explain their decision as a choice between the long struggles of legitimate life and a chance to earn quick and sometimes staggering amounts of cash. What follows are the accounts of three young crack dealers, how they entered the drug trade and how they ran their businesses.
>
> In some ways they are exceptional accounts. All three were ambitious and well organized when they started selling drugs. And even after they became crack addicts, they retained enough insight to realize that they had to escape the drug world to survive. . . .
>
> **The Young Entrepreneur**
> His was a crack business with a well-to-do clientele. Until he left the trade this year, at the age of twenty-one, he counted among his custom-

ers four doctors, a psychotherapist, a diamond merchant, and two very dependable police officers.

All told, there were forty people who knew the number of his telephone beeper. Business was conducted a few hours a day, from 6 P.M. to 9 P.M., when he drove around in a blue sports car, watching telephone numbers appear on the beeper, stopping at pay telephones and meeting his clients on street corners or at their apartments to sell them white rocks of cocaine. "I am selling a higher quality product, a much purer form of cocaine," he recalled telling his customers. "When you deal with me, there are no worries, because you are dealing with the best."

Although crack use is most widespread among the poor, experts said they believed that there was also an uncounted but significant number of middle-class users.

As he described his clients, the dealer's face broke into the sort of salesman's smile that in another place, with another product, might he considered quintessentially American. His dark eyes turned boyish. His voice, usually weighted with the diction of an old-time mobster, turned crisp . . . as a junior executive's.

Each night, he was buying a quarter of an ounce of cocaine for $300. He cooked it into crack in the basement of his mother's house, using her lasagna pan, and sold it for $600. He could have earned more than $300 a night, he says, but he found no reason to be "a greedy monster."

One evening, he recalled, he was called to the apartment of a customer, a Hasidic Jew, who had smoked all the cocaine he had bought with cash. Overwhelmed by his craving, the customer offered an antique gold menorah, a family heirloom.

"No, I won't take that," the dealer recalled saying, despite having taken gold chains, jewelry and videocassette recorders as payment in the past. "When the holidays come, you are going to look yourself in the mirror. And then what are you going to do, buy a plastic menorah at K-Mart?"

Like many drug dealers, he entered the business in a calculated way, first weighing the risks and the gains. And, like others, he decided drug dealing was too lucrative and too safe to resist.

He had been raised in Florida and Brooklyn by a Puerto Rican mother, who admonished him to pursue an honest career, and an Italian-American father, who had worked in low-level jobs for one of the five organized crime families of New York. The young man had always received good grades in school and imagined himself someday as a legitimate businessman with a college degree.

"I always expected to be a suit-and-tie kind of guy," he said. "But you have to go to college and you have to wait before you make real money. I wanted to put away a nest egg first."

At seventeen, he recalled, he and three other young men organized a marijuana-distribution location on a Brooklyn street corner. His part of the operation sold $8500 worth of marijuana a week. He paid each of his three salesmen $1000. Later, he said, he paid $1000 a week to a major Mafia figure for protection.

After a police crackdown on the corner, the dealers began a marijuana-delivery service, distributing a calling card printed with a beeper number and a marijuana cigarette as a trademark. Customers would dial the beeper and then their own phone numbers. The dealers would call back to arrange meeting places. By late 1985, cocaine replaced marijuana as their main product.

Meanwhile, he kept a daytime job with a construction business; lived with his mother, who knew nothing of his second career; and kept a list of his clients on his home computer. He also kept four guns locked in a safe, he said. But by last year, the competition was becoming stiff, and violence between crack dealers commonplace. He hired a body guard to accompany him on his deliveries. One night, he said, as he stood in front of a nightclub on a Brooklyn street corner, he heard a voice scream, "Watch out!"

As he turned his head, he saw another dealer, a competitor, lunge at him, swinging a baseball bat riddled with nails. He dove between two parked cars, but the nails tore into the back of one leg. The competitor drove off. Just before dawn, he said, his bodyguard found the assailant and shot him in the knees.

Several months later, the dealer's partner was shot to death, and the dealer realized that he was a crack addict himself, working just to support his habit. Several months ago, he left the business and entered treatment.

The Young Mother

Last January, she stood shivering outside a dilapidated Chinese restaurant, a crack dealer peddling $20 vials with a .38-caliber revolver tucked under her coat.

The crack business, once a free-for-all, where anyone with a frying pan and a source of cocaine powder could double money overnight, was being taken over by gangs with machine guns. But she still worked alone, a small woman, terrified, and with a brutal craving for cocaine to satisfy. She knew, she said, that unless she quit soon, she would probably be dead.

Just four years earlier, when a friend first offered her a job in the drug trade, her decision seemed perfectly logical. The business was the sole industry that would offer a high-paying job to a black mother on welfare. The threat of arrest seemed slight. And an alternative, a legitimate career that might lift her family out of poverty, just did not seem to exist.

"You can make more money than you have ever imagined," she recalled a friend as having told her, "just sitting in a bar selling packets of cocaine."

She was a twenty-year-old mother with a two-year-old child living in a public housing project. Each day, she said, she strained to make a weekly budget of $200, from welfare and her husband's tiny salary, cover rent, food, diapers and baby formula. At night, she would peer down on her sleeping daughter or stare out the window at the rows of boarded-up storefronts, roofs, and subway tracks that stretched to the horizon.

But her friend belonged to one of the successful families of the ghetto. His father was one of a generation of black entrepreneurs who had made a fortune in the numbers industry and invested the profits from illegal gambling in real estate all around the borough. To people in her neighborhood, she said, there are really two thriving industries from which real money can be made, numbers and drugs.

Her friend, a young man with an eye to the future, was beginning to invest some of his father's capital in the cocaine business. He had made contact with a ring of Cuban cocaine traffickers and was selling the drug in an unlicensed club the family owned in the neighborhood. He needed a pleasant salesperson. The pay was $300 to $400 a night.

In the club, a darkened disco with ear-splitting music, she sat on a bar stool. When customers approached, she said, she would take them to a restroom or alcove. Customers bought $20 packets of cocaine wrapped in aluminum foil.

The club flourished and soon she was a junior partner, employing nine dealers who sold cocaine in the club and outside on surrounding blocks. As she walked from her housing project to work each night, dozens of people would approach her, asking to buy drugs.

Now four gold rings adorned each hand. Her income was sometimes $1000 a night, and she dressed well, she recalled. But most of the money disappeared in the free drugs she gave to friends and into her own growing cocaine habit.

One night, in late 1985, she was standing outside the club when she saw nine plainclothes police offers jump out of cars and scramble through the front door. In the raid, her partner and six underlings were arrested. Although she was not caught, she only had a few dollars left in savings.

But crack was replacing the powdered form of the drug in New York, and she knew that for people who sold crack, making money was even more magical. Together with three friends, she purchased an eighth of an ounce of cocaine for $250, cooked it with baking soda in a frying pan, and sold it as fifty capsules for $500.

The next day the four bought more cocaine, cooked it into crack and sold $1000 worth of crack on the street. In five days, they had turned $250 into $7000.

"At that time, anybody who had crack could sell it," she said. "But then it got to a point where one guy who invested all his money and never got high would say, 'This is my corner.' "

The rules of the street suddenly changed. Death became the penalty for any transgression. And by this year, she said, more than twenty-five people she knew in the neighborhood had been shot to death in drug-related violence.

One day last winter, another dealer beat her severely with brass knuckles and slashed her face with a three-inch knife blade. She now rarely had time to see her daughter, whom her mother cared for. Six months ago, with her dreams of a new life lost long ago, she decided to enter a treatment program, far from the battleground she knew as home.

The Jamaican Mafia

It is not hard to make a fortune running two locations to sell crack, the twenty-six-year-old dealer said, speaking with a light Caribbean lilt. Just follow a few simple rules, and, when necessary, do not hesitate to use your gun.

He had joined a subculture of Jamaican immigrants who established themselves in the marijuana business in New York in the mid-seventies and, in the last two years, have become some of the most successful and violent street distributors of the smokable form of cocaine.

To neighbors in his middle-class neighborhood in Brooklyn, he recalls, he appeared to be a stable businessman with a pleasant family. He commuted to work in Manhattan each morning, maintained a tidy home and appeared to love playing with his children in the evenings. His legitimate job, in fact, was real. But on his way home from work at night, he said, he stopped at two Brooklyn apartments in buildings where the superintendents had been generously paid off. At each apartment the knobs had been ripped out of the front door, and customers stood in line in the hallways to pass cash through the holes in exchange for vials of crack.

He would drop off a new shipment of the drug, and the two employees in each apartment would hand him the day's earnings.

"My nice neighbors just thought of me as a regular Jamaican guy, looking good, dressing good," he said. "See, I am careful not to put myself in a position to get busted. I've never been busted yet."

The dealer had learned the ways of the drug trade from his older brother, another immigrant from Kingston, who avoided taking drugs himself, owns nine apartment buildings, he said, and has a tax-free income of more than $300,000 a year.

His father had been a successful engineer who urged his son to find legitimate work. But his older brother was involved with the highly organized and well-financed marijuana-smuggling organizations, which he called the Jamaican Mafia. At seventeen, he told his brother that he, too, wanted to join the business.

"I was saying, 'The cars they have, the clothes they have, why not me?' " he recalled. " 'I want some of the things they've got. I want in.' "

After proving that he could peddle packets of marijuana on the street, he recalled, his brother showed him how superintendents of buildings could be bought for $300 every two weeks and how marijuana, double-wrapped in plastic and smuggled in luggage through customs on flights from Kingston, could be purchased at $500 a pound and sold in $10, $45, and $60 packets for $4000.

The income from his brother's two marijuana locations brought him $1200 a week income, which he supplemented with $300 from his regular job. He invested some money to buy a house and lavish cars, jewelry, and clothing, but he reported to the government solely the income from his legitimate job.

Like many drug dealers, he said, the brothers found the profits and quick turnover of the crack trade irresistible.

One night, he said, as he waited to enter a sales apartment, two armed men jumped him and hurled him through the half-open door. His employees, however, were quick to react. They opened fire first, wounding an intruder. Later, they dumped his blood-soaked body on a nearby street. The second intruder fled.

For Jamaicans in the street crack trade, he said, shootouts quickly became an expected part of the business.[5]

From these interviews with drug dealers, addicts, and ex-addicts, and from all the previous money talk from gamblers, prostitutes, and thieves, it becomes clear that any form of morality becomes secondary to their compulsions to acquire more and more money to solve their emotional feelings of low self-esteem.

It is evident that it's not just cash that they are after, but more what the cash is equivalent to in their minds. John Irwin describes theft as a crime of emotional revenge, designed to retaliate against an unjust society. To many petty criminals, money is vengeance. To professional crime masters like Albie Baker, money is glamor; to white collar criminals, money is power. For prostitutes, money can range from being the measure of emotional self-worth to being a means of meting out punishment to men to make up for past emotional abuse. For gamblers, money is the thrill of the action, much like the fix a junkie gets from shooting dope.

In all of the contexts, throughout deviant subcultures and lifestyles, money is at the root of much illicit activity and illegal activity is a recurrent theme. For all these individuals, the acquisition of money is an effort to compensate for their emotional deprivations in their lives that has created feelings of low self-esteem. Money, and its power, however, doesn't adequately fill the emotional hole in their lives. Their deviant lives generally involve the insatiable pursuit of cash, and their emotional emptiness is only temporarily resolved by the money they acquire.

CHAPTER

9

The Helping Professions and Money

$\mathcal{A}$S A THERAPIST, sociologist, criminologist, researcher, and university professor, I have personally learned a great deal about the role of money in the helping professions. These occupations are supposed to be dedicated to helping people rather than for profit. One particular experience I had vividly epitomizes the peculiar monetary dilemmas people in these fields face with money-oriented clients.

In my work, my wife and I have taken "problem" teenagers into our home over the years, in cases where parents felt the teen was beyond control. In one such instance, a troubled sixteen-year-old, the son of a super-wealthy businessman, came to live with us one summer. As autumn came onto the horizon, the issue of public or private school for the fall term came up. The young man, my wife, as co-therapist, and I came to the conclusion that a particular private school would be a better option than a public one, since the youth would have a more intimate school setting. We arranged a meeting with his millionaire father at our house to discuss the issue, making certain the teenager would not be there when we laid out our plan to his father.

The father, a multimillionaire, saw the logic of a private school immediately, but he told us, "I've set a limited budget for my son's care, and that's all I will pay." He put to us a compromise. He was willing to share in paying for the private school tuition if we reduced our monthly charge for keeping the young man. He reasoned out loud, "After all, you are in the business of helping people, I'm not."

Even though the youth was *his* son, not *ours,* he saw no reason to suspend his business-is-business approach to life. And he expected me as a professional helper to, in a sense, "put my money where my humanitarian mouth was."

After some negotiation, my wife and I agreed to drop our modest monthly room, board, and therapy charge by about $150 for the sake of the boy. The father was delighted with the deal. Then he invited us outside to take a look at a brand-new $150,000 Corniche Rolls-Royce, purchased that very afternoon, apparently seeing nothing incongruous about doing so just after having chopped our fee. When I brought up to him what was for me a paradox, his smiling response was, "Hey, you're a therapist and a humanitarian, I'm a businessman."

This little tale of conflict, manipulation, and inconsistency is a metaphor for the relationship between money and people involved in the helping professions: therapists, doctors, researchers, teachers, to name a few. Somehow the vocation to help, to heal, to teach, is seen by many people as a charitable avocation, not a business. There is the clear implication that people who help people should be pure-bred idealists, above mundane materialistic concerns. The business side of the business of helping others is seen by many people as inappropriate. What's forgotten is the obvious fact that people who help people need money too. They have to earn a living.

Society is filled with examples of this odd bias. Teachers are not supposed to want higher pay; their business is motivating students. Nurses aren't supposed to strike despite low-paying, high-stress, understaffed hospitals. Sick people deserve medical care and doctors should give it free, if necessary. Psychological therapy, too, should be dispensed with regard to who has coverage. Social workers should focus on their caseloads, not their pay stubs. It's fine for business people to be focused on "making it," and making money, but such goals are considered by many to be unethical for professional helpers.

Many helpers bow to this attitude and often take less pay than they should for their services. They struggle with the issue of money for help as they set fees and try to collect. Many people in the helping field are afflicted with an inner tug of war between altruism, guilt, and materialism. Throughout this chapter the money talk of professional helpers will demonstrate how each has faced and handled the money issue and its multifaceted personal and professional implications.

Ann Landers is a renowned columnist who has helped millions with her advice. She speaks openly here about how she entered the helping profession and some of the emotional issues related to the helping professions and money. Following is the interview I had with her in her home in Chicago.

"I came from an upper middle class Midwestern Jewish family, raised during the Depression. My father had done quite well. We had everything we needed. We were never hungry. I make that statement remembering that a great many kids were. I remember when my mother used to pack lunches for us, she'd always put in several extra sandwiches and say, 'Look, maybe there'll be somebody there who doesn't have enough.' We never brought home a thing. Everything that went in that sack, somebody wanted.

"My mother taught me how to be compassionate. She was a person who was concerned about other people. I never would have thought to bring sandwiches if Mother hadn't suggested it. Her concern was something that, very early, made an impact on me.

"Being one of a twin, we shared. [Dear Abby is Ann Landers's twin sister.] We talked about things. It was sort of double exposure to everything that happened.

"We had a modest allowance and we saved most of it. I remember streetcars at that time were a nickel a ride. And we lived about a mile from downtown. While we certainly didn't need to save a nickel—particularly when it was bitter cold—we would walk from downtown with our violin cases. We went downtown to take a violin lesson. We would walk to save the nickel, so that two nickels made a dime and we would save our money and buy Mother something for Mother's Day, or buy a present for somebody. The money always seemed to go for somebody else. So as I look back in retrospect, that was quite a generous thing for kids to do.

"After having come from a comfortable family, what did I do but marry a young man who had absolutely no money. In fact, he borrowed three hundred dollars to get married on. But I felt that he was very promising, very bright, very worthwhile, and had all the things that I wanted in a husband, and it never occurred to me that this was risky, to marry a man who didn't have any money. I was quite sure that he would be a success. It never occurred to me that he wouldn't. He would make it. We worked shoulder to shoulder. I never had an outside job because I had a child the first year I was married, and that took care of that, but it just seemed that it was imperceptible, his progress. It seemed every six months we'd be moving to another city because he was able to make a little more money at another job. He would be promoted, and this is the way it happened. And the next thing I knew, he was making very good money, but those things happen in a way that you don't perceive them while they're happening to you. It's just like when someone says, 'My God, I'm forty pounds overweight.' Well, at no time did you realize this was happening. You just suddenly wake up to the fact that there you are—and that's how we became quite wealthy.

"I changed from Eppie Lederer to Ann Landers when we moved to Chicago. I never thought I would ever work. I had never had a job before. I had had absolutely no experience. The opportunity to have this column came along. I accepted it with all the chutzpah you can imagine, being green as grass, never having published a line, knowing nothing about newspapers or writing.

"I thought this work would be a marvelous opportunity to help a great number of people who actually had no place to go with their problems. It seemed to me when people are reduced to writing to a stranger, to an advice column, they must be pretty desperate. There must be millions of those people out there who have nobody to talk to.

"Money didn't mean a thing to me when I began this column, partly because my husband and I were already millionaires. I started with $100 a week. I felt it was a blessing. I didn't need the money. I was delighted with the opportunity to help people.

"People agonize about people problems, not money problems.

Money often becomes the pivotal basis for the argument. Money is the excuse, the straw man they put up. What they're arguing about is something quite different. Money is a respectable point on which people can differ. It's something they both understand. They can be arguing about money and it's okay, but the hostility and the anger is really rooted someplace else.

"Another aspect of the money thing is the way people act when they get involved with wills. Benjamin Franklin said, 'If you would like to know the true character of a person, share an inheritance with him.' That, to me, was an astute observation, because I do hear about this in my mail. People aren't writing to me to tell me they're hard up. The 'money mail' is often on the subject of wills, about what happens through conflicts in their family. I remember one letter that went like this: 'I thought my brothers were decent and my sisters were marvelous and so were my aunts and uncles. Well, when my mother died, you should have seen the vultures. Everybody came and fought. This one wanted the ring. Where are the earrings? Wasn't there a pin?'

"Ben Franklin had rare insights. I cannot believe that people could care so strongly about things and money to fight to the death with relatives over the monetary remains of a dead person. Apparently these people who are hung up on things are emotionally poverty-stricken in a very important way. At the heart of themselves, they must be very empty and they're trying to fill up this emptiness with acquisitions, with things.

"This to me is an old story. I know so many people who have great wealth and are miserable. They've missed it all. They don't know what life is all about. They don't feel good about themselves, good about their relationships with other people. They are often lonely and friendless. When some kind of terrible disappointment or tragedy comes along, they have nothing to bounce back with. They have no inner resources. I see this all around me. They often forget the people they knew back when, when they didn't have anything.

"Millionaires? I wouldn't generalize about millionaires as a category any more than I would about musicians or doctors, because you have to look at each person as an individual. Some are marvelously generous and have a great social conscience. Then there are some who are self-serving, stingy. It depends on the millionaires you are talking about.

"If you're asking me, 'What does money mean to me?'—money is something I can make because I was lucky enough to get into a field where there is money to be made. I don't think money gives me or anyone else special status. I would hate to think that anyone was interested in me either because of my work, or my fame as Ann Landers, or because I have money. In fact, I don't allow my friends to call me Ann, they call me Eppie. I don't want to get Ann and Eppie mixed up. I want to know who I am and I want them to know who I am. If they're interested in Ann Landers, then they'd better go someplace else.

"The most important and satisfying thing in my life isn't money, it's what I inherited from my mother—the drive and, fortunately, the ability to help people with their problems. I really don't need money. My husband and I are millionaires.

"My work has made it possible for me to have fame, fortune, and perform a public service. I didn't have to make any choice between these alternatives. but if I had to make a choice, I would without question choose a life of public service, because that's where the gratification is. That's where the fun is."

Many helping professionals would like to be in Ann Lander's position, able to focus solely on humanitarian pursuits and not concern themselves with money. However, their own personal supply side economics demands they face up to earning money. The bottom line for helping professionals is that they are in a business that must support them, their needs and those of their families.

Many humanitarians would like to forget about the business side of life. In reality, they can afford to no less than any business person can. Drumming up profitable business is an occupational necessity. Dr. H. is a prime example of a professional humanitarian who didn't put enough time into the business side of his profession, and now has some regrets.

Dr. H. is fifty-two, holds a Ph.D. in business and economics (ironically), and is currently doing independent research into evolutionary theory and the evolution of social systems. He prepares articles for various scientific journals. Although he is diligently, ambitiously, and selflessly contributing to the body of scientific knowledge, no single employer is contributiing to his bank account. And though the world may benefit in the long run from his intellectual pursuits, Dr. H. has seen limited short-run earnings for too long. Money for Dr. H. was always a philosophical issue, until he found himself broke and (from a financial standpoint) unemployed.

"It's depressing for me to have to go down to the unemployment office and look at the people who are labeled 'misfits,' 'dregs' of society. Many of them haven't the faintest idea why they're unemployed or what their problems are. When you have to do this, you really have to steel yourself for it.

"I've concluded, based on my recent personal experiences as a poor person, that the best way to be happy is to have some materialistic, monetarily secure position and be relatively closed with regard to your mind and intellectual process. The more closed your mind, the more chance that you will be in a relatively high-paying, secure position, and the less aware you will be of how all kinds of things fit together or ought to fit together. The more open your mind and viewpoint in modern society, the more you see the follies and foibles and the more discontented you are with it. The open mind asks 'why' and 'what could be done?' and all that is a potentially nonhappy thing to do. The happiness you get from asking these types of questions is all internal and not something you get from the outside, or from money.

"I'm aware that if I had money and the position and power that went with it, it might be my undoing—it might prevent me from doing the work that I think is important. Yet knowing this, I can probably be bought. If I was offered $100,000 for a position in a planning office in a defense industry, I might take it.

"Given my humanistic and philosophical position, I totally disapprove of the military killer complex. Yet my recent lack of money and the pain of going down to that unemployment office and facing those people has changed me. Like many other people in this country, I've recently discovered I can be bought."

PSYCHOTHERAPISTS AND MONEY

Drumming up money is still an occupational necessity, even if one is in the business of therapeutically helping others. The area of psychotherapy is one of the most interesting grounds in which to explore the relationship between helpers, helping, and money. Psychologists, psychiatrists, and counselors are in the business of helping people emotionally. Since this is a paid service, money plays a starring, dramatic, and controversial role. Questions range from simple ones of fee scales to more complicated philosophical issues. Is higher-priced therapy more effective? Should therapy be free? Should therapists themselves share in the cost? Does the economic exchange between client and therapist influence the emotional exchange and progress? Does money itself become a therapeutic issue? The following interviews with several psychotherapists explore these issues.

The old "you get what you pay for" adage often applies to therapy, at least from the point of view of many clients. For some people the two-hundred-dollars-an hour therapist is better, four times better, than the fifty-dollars-an-hour therapist. Given the fact that a number of studies reveal that high expectations of being treated successfully at the start of therapy are more significant than the doctor's methods, some people impressed by the fee will respond with more positive emotions to the higher priced therapist than the "cheaper" one.

Some therapists disagree with this notion. Dr. George Bach, internationally respected psychologist and author of landmark books like *Group Psychotherapy, The Intimate Enemy, and Creative Aggression,* presented some fascinating remarks on therapy, money, and the connection between the two when I interviewed him at his home.

"I'm aware and knowledgeable about the concept of charging people more or less in terms of their psychological needs. For some people, if you charge them too little, they don't think much of you. Hence, it's not good for their therapy. You should, according to this view, charge them more. The more you charge, the better the therapy. But that's nonsense. I've worked in state hospitals, in clinics, and I've known poor patients who respond beautifully to therapy where no money changed hands. The price doesn't count. It depends on your skill at motivating the person, although sometimes the therapeutic fee is highly significant, especially for a client who has money as an emotional problem.

"Dr. Carl Rogers has an interesting viewpoint on therapy and money. At a recent conference he gave a talk saying he personally felt that money—having to pay or be paid—puts you at a disadvantage in psychotherapy because it puts you as a service. 'You are, in fact, a hired hand. The client is hiring you, you don't have equality.' Of course, he has a point.

"Despite this, however, I find that people try to bribe me a lot with money. For example, one husband in a marital conflict wanted to avoid divorce, and he wanted me to dissuade his wife from divorcing him. So, he subtly tried to give me money, impress me with his power or affluence. There is often this unconscious bribing by a display of wealth so I'll 'go easy' on him, and perhaps persuade his wife that she should stay with him.

"In another case, I had this millionaire's daughter from Beverly Hills as a client. The father wanted me to straighten her out psychologically—his way. He wanted me to give his daughter his viewpoint on life. He paid me well, and he wanted me to be beholden to him, to be his agent with his daughter. I angered him by refusing to go along with his game plan.

"Of course, over the years I have treated a whole generation of people in Beverly Hills who were castrated by their parents' money. The hardest cases have been the second-generation rich because they are told by the first, 'I made it.' He made it first, up from poverty, even though he was actually a part of a sociocultural development. The second generation son or daughter feels they can't duplicate their parents' wealth, success, or eminence. There are exceptions, but rarely. They react by doing nothing, in which case they get to me because they get into the drug scene and give up. Or, they become rip-off artists. They were castrated, hanging around, scared to death of going out on their own. Many settle to be losers. They go along hoping that their parents will remain generous. Their parents hold onto them with money.

"I have a case now, a patient who gets money from her wealthy father only when she's emotionally ill, even if it's psychosomatic. When she's sick a lot of money is there. The rent's paid, she gets everything. So, she gets sick a lot. It's one of my failure cases. I cannot make much progress, and it drives me bananas, because the moment I make progress and she gets on her own, the money is withdrawn. So, when she gets partially well, she is withdrawn from me, from therapy. I've forbidden her to stop therapy, and I see her on a reduced basis. This case is not atypical.

"Many Hollywood stars like me as a therapist because I'm not overly impressed by them or their fame. Most stars, by the way, are ripped off right and left. They're great money makers, but horrible money managers. I have psychologically worked on their star issues. Many of these people do not feel deserving of the large amounts of money they receive. They get rid of it as fast as they get it. They usually have a low opinion of themselves in the first place. The ones I see are extremely masochistic, and allow themselves to be victimized by unscrupulous managers and leeches. They are like guilty, crooked gamblers who can't stand their financial success so they get rid of the money as fast as they can.

"Money to me personally is a heavy subject, you know. I've steered away from confronting it too, realistically. My mother considered money to be evil because she herself came from a noble but poor family. To her, poverty and ethics went together and she believed wealth corrupted. Even though I'm a psychologist, I am not immune to the trip she laid on me. I grew up in a wealthy family, although my father was the poorest of our wealthy relatives. In my youth, the smell of money was all around us. I felt a sense of relief and pride when I started out on my own, a young man literally penniless. I love to tell the story of how I rose, how I made my fellowships, how I worked my ass off as a laborer, and enjoyed it. To this day, everything I have could burn down, I wouldn't be afraid. I can see myself learning how to work once again on a low salary. Money isn't that important to me.

"I discovered one thing as a psychologist about rich people who make big money. They are usually simple personalities. They smell one thing, a loser, and they smell a winner. And they use that discretionary power. It doesn't matter where it leads them, they stick to it.

"Basically, money in a person's life is either central or tangential. If it's tangential, a person can roll either way. If he's rich, he won't be overly impressed with being rich. He won't be overly scared shitless by being poor. If money is central, he is at the mercy of this financial thing, he will keep track of it and is controlled by it. That's a sorry state of being.

"Regarding bill payments, I have most people pay me cash on the barrelhead. I don't let them get too far into owing me for my services. I make my patients pay me visit by visit. I used to let the payment go too far and it pissed me off, and negatively affected my relationship with my patients. I still often get bankruptcy notes. Some of the wealthiest patients, world famous stars, gyp me. I struggled with this problem a lot, because at first I thought it was undignified for me to ask for payment. Then, I decided my anger and their negative guilt negatively affected the therapeutic process more than if I came out and made them pay cash on the barrelhead.

"Most of the guys on Bedford Drive [Beverly Hills, Freud's Alley] are in the marketplace, count their money and go across the street to invest and play the stock market. Money is extremely important to most of my psychologist friends. In fact, one of them recently quit being a psychoanalyst and became vice-president of a bank.

"Money is crucial to them. You can get them to talk at lunch more easily about their latest investments than you could get them to talk about psychoanalytic theory, which is what I always want to talk bout. I am considered a pain in the ass. 'Oh, here comes George. Christ, now we're going to have to listen to his latest theories on aggression and group therapy.' And they say to me, 'Don't you ever relax?'

"In my practice I've noted several aspects of the emotional value of money. One thing that's striking is how little people in therapy are willing to talk about money. In particular, they will seldom tell you how much they're worth. A person will tell you their most bizarre sexual practices or heinous crimes or terrible things they've done to other people. They'll reveal terrible issues from the depth of their soul, but they'll never spontaneously tell you how much they're worth. And if you pointedly ask them, many will say, 'That's my business.'"

Many people in psychotherapeutic practice find that the pressure of society's expectation that their motives will be solely humanitarian and the reality of having to run a business add up to inner conflict. In addition to the need to organize and run a business, many in this field have to reorganize their values. An inner tug of war ensues between idealism and humanitarianism on the one hand and materialism on the other. Feelings of self-doubt, guilt, and betrayal were articulated by many therapists I interviewed.

Len, a social worker, reflected these complicated feelings in describing his emotional relationship to money and how money issues affected his becoming a social worker.

"My family was poor. My most poignant memory of this happened after the stock market crash in '29. My father, who worked in a warehouse all his life, lost his job. He used to go down to the park and sit there on a park bench with his head bowed down. That picture of him is etched in my memory. I was seven at the time.

"It taught me two things—I could wind up on that loser's bench someday no matter how much money I made, and secondly, I developed a strong feeling of compassion for good poor people and wanted to help them.

"Why should my father be in that spot? It wasn't his fault. Early on, I saw how ridiculous social conditions could put a good person in a terrible life situation, like my unemployed father. Another thing I thought to myself was how can I have fun, even as a kid, when I'm reminded that there's someone out there broke and unhappy like my father. Seeing my father on that park bench flat broke set me up as someone who wanted to help people. I felt sorry for him and his pain, but as a kid I couldn't do anything about it. When I became an adult I realized there were lots of people like my old man. I trained myself and now I'm somewhat capable of relieving the pain of poverty, at least for some people.

"The happiest and most emotionally ecstatic experience I have ever had with money revolved around a period in my teenage years when I was a kind of lightweight dice hustler. I hung out with a gang of these hustlers, older guys. We would clock a guy for his money, figure whether he was holding $50 or $100. Winning the money was a sweet experience for a fifteen-year-old kid. I'd take a shot with dice that gave you a percentage, or we'd use crooked kinds of dice. We always won. It was especially fun to beat a wise guy. I had no mercy in those days. I later learned in my therapy why I enjoyed being the hustler rather than the victim. Symbolically, my father was a mark, a victim. I enjoyed being the hustler because it was a better role in life. If I was on top, I wouldn't be on the bottom. I wouldn't be like my long-suffering father.

"Money is a factor in my marriage. As you notice, I live in a nice house. I would live very frugally if I were single, probably a small apartment on the beach in Venice. But I want my kid to live in a nice house. My wife has to live well because of early problems with being poor. In many respects I am pushed by her needs, because when you're married you should respect the needs of the other person.

"Yet one of my biggest fights with my wife revolves around money. She always thinks her situation is not as good as she'd like to have it. I personally feel I live better than I should. For example, when I have a poor client come to me for therapy here at my office in my house, I feel a little sheepish living in this big house. I feel if I'm going to be talking with enthusiasm about what people ought to do about their problems, I ought to be living as I used to, in a leaner financial situation. I feel I would then be more entitled to talk abut social problems than I am now, living in relative affluence.

"Despite this, money, to me, is freedom. Right now, if I had a hundred thousand in the bank, I would take my wife and kid and spend a week on the French Riviera. I would just do that. At the same time, I've known people who had all the money in the world and killed themselves because [they felt] life wasn't worth anything. Based on my own life experience and my social work, I'm absolutely convinced that money has an enormous effect on a person's emotional condition."

DOCTORS, DENTISTS, AND MONEY

In Len's case, early money-related experience "drove" him into a humanitarian occupation, and he has conflicts about being financially successful. Karl is a fifty-year-old medical doctor whose life experience reveals some additional issues on how and why people in the helping professions relate to money.

He reported: "My parents were poor when they came over to this country from Vienna. They never had a lot of money. Both worked, but somehow I never felt poor because my mother would literally take the food out of her mouth in order to feed me. She would sew my clothes and always made me presentable. I had long overcoats and things like that, which were really out of fashion. I felt like a creep, but as far as bare necessities, I never felt like I was going to starve. As I grew older, I became aware that some kids were rich and some kids were poor.

"I never felt envious, and I didn't feel inferior. I felt they had more money than I did, but I felt I was smarter than they were. I had a strong sense of myself. Fuck them, they were just lucky.

"Now, as a doctor, I'm rich and one of the enemy I used to despise. The first year I earned $100,000, it was just incredible. It was income tax time and I added up the figure two and three times to make sure I hadn't made a mistake! I feel generally, at gut level, that there's something wrong with being wealthy. That you can't be wealthy and do it honestly and honorably. It means exploiting other people somehow.

"In my practice I have a standard fee for a visit, but I'm flexible. Those who can pay it do, and other people pay less. I suppose my attitudes about the rich were formed early in my life. I don't gouge them, but I get back at them with a bigger fee. The poor are charged less, and rightly so. If I had a million I would finance a free medical clinic of some kind that would provide poor people with excellent medical services."

Charles is a forty-six-year-old surgeon who has found a recent financial crunch is exacerbating his inner turmoil over his values and money. "Right now, money is the most important thing in the world to me. I just spent a fortune for a quarter's malpractice insurance, which is exactly triple what I paid just two years ago. I've put myself in a financial hole for the first time in my life because I closed my practice for six weeks during a so-called malpractice crisis. Because of that I am going to be getting only a trickle of money in the next few weeks. That bothers me, because I have had to become a businessman for the first time since I went into practice fifteen years ago!

"I never used to think that money affected me emotionally. I always took it for granted, never gave it much thought. Now all of a sudden my insurance triples and the money stops coming in and I'm in hot water.

"Money was always secondary in the work I do. I like the feeling of helping people, and in my line of work you have the opportunity to do that on a daily basis. It was very rewarding to me personally.

"One of my major concerns is that this overextension of my finances has compromised my ethics. I have always looked at my work as a humanitarian field that gave me a great deal of satisfaction. I always deplored and have been critical of the businessman doctors. Now I'm doing a lot of self-examination about the fact that maybe I've become what I've always hated—a businessman doctor!"

"I was dedicated to my profession and I was involved with my patients and their health. Now I have to admit it, when a patient comes in and they have a lot of money, they get special attention."

[Have you ever performed a surgical operation just for the money?] "That's a vicious question. Of course not. But I'll tell you, in borderline cases, when the patient is rich, maybe I am swayed into earning several thousand dollars in an afternoon."

[Do some surgeons perform surgery on patients who don't really need it?] "Of the doctors I've known over the years, I would put it this way. There are three categories of surgeons. Category one would be highly ethical professionals who meticulously analyze each case, even, if necessary, get a second opinion, and then make a decision that is devoid of the monetary-gain factor. The second category consists of doctors who do their research, and if it's borderline and enough money is involved, do the operation. The third category is comprised of butchers who will operate on almost anyone for the money. These psychopathic doctors are superrich. Where would I put myself in these categories? I used to be in category one, but because of my financial problems, I've moved into category two. Money now counts in my role as a doctor."

Dentistry is another helping professional role that can set up role conflicts in the practitioner on the emotional meaning of money. Irv is a dentist who has had conflicts on the money issue in his work. At the age fifty-three, he became a millionaire, due to real estate investments he had made to supplement his dental practice income. His interview reveals his money ethics, and how he feels about making it financially.

"The worst I've ever felt about doing something for money alone happened the first year I was in dental practice. I was working for a guy for $2 an hour, twenty hours a week and I was seeing my own patients too. In 1945 my goal was $100 a week. There was a hygienist who was making more than me and I was a dentist. So on that basis I asked for more money. He went and cut her salary to give me a raise. She came in and chewed me out. I wanted to crawl under a rock.

"I've never had any marital conflict over money because I've never said no to my wife. One Sunday in the San Fernando Valley it was a hundred degrees and Muriel said something like, 'You're a dentist and you're doing well, why can't we have a swimming pool?', I said, 'Fine, you'll have a swimming pool.' Monday morning I called in the order. It was the wrong time for me; I didn't have much money, but I worked it out somehow.

"Money was always a more complicated matter to me in my work situation than at home with my family. For example, there are always dental decisions that are made on the basis of money. If somebody comes in and you got a three-unit bridge and there's decay and it's leaking, then you got two decisions to make. You can clean it out and repair it . . . [or you can] remake that bridge entirely. . . . You can make a hell of a case for an $800 repair or a $75 temporary repair. At that point, you ask yourself, Am I doing this bridge because it's more profitable for me, or am I doing it because the patient really needs it?

"A patient had a problem where, in brief, I could have made a two- or three-unit bridge. Obviously, I would have made more money on the larger bridge. The patient had coverage that would pay for the a three-unit bridge. Just for the hell of it, I took the X-rays to two other dentists. What would they do? Both guys would put in the three-unit porcelain. Now, I don't know whether their professional judgment stem from sheer honesty or just that it's more profitable. But I can see where a young dentist with a heavy mortgage to pay would go for the three-unit bridge! Now that I'm richer, maybe my humanitarian standards are rising.

"I don't believe there are dentists who would drill an unnecessary cavity for cash; on the other hand, some dentists overtreat. Money plays an important role in dentistry." Obviously, Irv is one of the more ethical dentists in America.

Businessman and professional helper are often seen as contradictory roles by both the professionals and their clients. The helping professional, unlike people strictly in a money-making profession, is not supposed to become a profiteer. It's almost as if society has a special rule about conflict of interest directed at helping professionals which says idealism and profit can't mix. So many in the medical fields, in the intellectual ivory towers, and in the mental health disciplines are torn by the conflict between their values, the challenge of making a living and justifying it at the same time. Money becomes a double-edged sword, not a very good weapon for those expected to help society combat its many ills and injustices. The challenge for the professional helper is to set up a balance between a reasonable earning power and the humanitarian motives which brought them into the helping professions. In this balancing process, they have to develop a monetary price that they feel is appropriate for their social conscience and their clients' well-being. Their emotions about money tend to affect their business practices in a complex way.

10

The Creative Arts, Talent and Money

When bankers dine together they discuss art.
When artists dine together they discuss money.
— Oscar Wilde

*F*OR MANY people the acquisition, saving, and growth of their wealth by wise investment is a primary drive in life. For others, people with some special talent or artistic ability, money and wealth are side effects of their creative motivation to perform effectively in their field. Bankers, people in real estate, agents, businessmen are obvious examples of people focused more on earning money than creative expression or community service.

On the other hand writers, actors, athletes, artists, and musicians are people who concentrate on their professional activities, derive great joy from their occupation, with money usually considered to be a secondary element if not a complicating factor in their lifestyle. In fact, people with some special talent who are focused on money rather than on their craft are often derisively viewed as *sellouts*.

Over the years, few stereotypes have remained as unvarying and as true as that of the "struggling artist." The struggle has traditionally been romanticized as the apprenticeship and delay necessary before the difficult and unique vision of the artist can penetrate the consciousness of the larger society. The artist is venerated for his or her self-sacrifice and dedication.

Part of the struggling artist image is the fact that poor artists or writers focused on their craft are often considered purer than those who have made it financially. Whether it's sour grapes or the stereotypical romantic image of the writer or artist starving in a garret—the public projects a level of sellout rumor onto financially successful professionals. Somehow they are "in it for the money"—and that's not the same thing as being a writer or artist consumed with being a creative artist.

For a person essentially involved with their art or talent, the issue of money can become a complicating factor. It is often suggested that the elimination of the issue of monetary reward could purify and totally focus the artist's involvement with his work. Although a project's potential monetary gain often spurs the production of a significant venture, many fine works of art have emanated from a monetary motivation. Many of the most remarkable paintings of the Renaissance were produced on the crass basis of money provided by wealthy supporters of the arts.

In an interview I had with the award-winning playwright Howard Sackler ("The Great White Hope"), he analyzed the money foundation of what is perhaps the greatest and most produced play in history, "Hamlet." In my interview with Sackler, who was an authority on Shakespeare, I commented on how money must have been a complicating problem for a writer like Shakespeare. He rebutted this allegation by describing in some detail the manner in which the production of "Hamlet" was motivated by the money force. Sackler, a student of Shakespeare for many years, commented: "In my analysis of the history of Shakespeare's 'Hamlet,' I found it was a project motivated by a group of businessmen who felt it would be a lucrative endeavor. Shakespeare joined the project because at the time he needed money."

WRITERS AND THE MONEY FACTOR

The life and career of F. Scott Fitzgerald are almost a metaphor for all the struggles afflicting writers when money is pitted against creativity. The importance of hard, cold cash above raw talent was a lesson young Scott learned early on from his grand amour, Zelda. She refused to marry him on the grounds that he was doing poorly financially, despite his pledges he was going to make it as a writer. Discouraged, he left his job and returned home to St. Paul, Minnesota, to write *This Side of Paradise,* which he sold to a publisher for a $5000 advance, enough money, in those days, to win and marry Zelda. Yet, he was scarred by this trial.

He wrote, "During a long summer of despair I wrote a novel instead of letters, so it came out all right, but it came out for a different person. The man with the jingle of money in his pocket who married the girl a year later would always cherish an abiding distrust, an animosity toward the leisure class."

The marriage was off to a questionable start. Fitzgerald's early financial success didn't last. High-style living in wild roaring-twenties fashion, drinking to excess, and partying has long been blamed for dissipating Fitzgerald's genius. Money was a constant source of family conflict and literary sabotage. Fitzgerald had to write "magazine trash" to pay the bills, leaving less time and creative energy for his main love— writing novels. Was celebrity, too much too soon, a harbinger of creative disaster? Torn between bill collectors and his editor, Maxwell Perkins, Fitzgerald led a poignant, tortured existence. He was the prototypical starving artist, one step ahead of the poorhouse, while trying hard not to betray his literary gift. He died with a deep sense of failure. Only in retrospect have his works been given proper homage, even the ones he wrote almost strictly for money like the Pat Hobby stories.

Fitzgerald was dogged by that burdensome choice: to write for economic gain or for artistic glory. The bottom line was clear: "Trash" turned a profit, literature did not. Writing commercial trash was the price one had to pay in order to create literature. In Fitzgerald's day the place to cash in on trash was Hollywood. He was not the first nor the last to head West, to sell out in order to finance literary aspirations later on.

In fact, the road to Hollywood is paved with the wasted energy of many brilliant writers, including Faulkner and Ernest Hemingway.

The choice Fitzgerald faced, trash versus art, still faces contemporary writers—now it's bestsellers as opposed to serious literature. Making a choice still requires writers to pay a price.

In the context of modern-day book publishing, consider a hypothetical, though often real, case. A writer has two offers from a publisher: to write Book A or Book B. He is twice as interested in writing Book A and would certainly enjoy it more. However, the drawback is that Book A has half the commercial appeal; Book B offers double the advance money since it has higher earning potential. The writer goes with Book B because, frankly, he's not financially secure enough to ignore the money.

Inevitably, "selling out" has emotional repercussions, mainly regrets and resentments. The writer tries to rationalize writing Book B, investing it with more value than it has. In the end, he justifies the decision with a pledge to write Book A with the profits from "prostituting" himself in the act of doing Book B.

Money controls and distorts creative decisions, rendering many of them impossible. A writer is damned if he writes for art's sake and goes broke in the process, and damned if he doesn't—opting for profit at the expense of becoming a "hack." No wonder few writers feel totally satisfied about their productions, and the process of writing.

Author Irving Shulman was one who successfully walked the tightrope, balancing bestsellers with creative satisfaction. *The Amboy Dukes* was a money-maker, while *Harlow* and others were less successful financially but acclaimed by critics. Another book of his became the classic film *Rebel Without a Cause*. Here's what he says about his rise to fame, his formula for literary success, and the emotional impact of money on his writing.

"I grew up in Brooklyn. My father had been a skilled mechanic in the hand-knot trade, doing specialty items—sweaters, hats, suits—which were expensive. In fact, he made a sweater for President Wilson, a very special sweater he helped design. Then the Depression hit. No one wanted special hand-made sweaters anymore. All this affected me personally, because I had never really thought in terms of money.

"I was thirty-three, working for the State Department in Washington, when I finished *The Amboy Dukes*. I got the idea from an incident that triggered my interest. A high school teacher had been shot dead by two students and I read about it in the papers. I said to myself, Why don't I write a book about that? I wasn't thinking about financial rewards, I was intrigued with the story.

"My idea of financial rewards was becoming a screenwriter in Hollywood. I had heard big stories about it and about how marvelous the movies were. I thought this book might do it for me. I wrote five pages a day come hell or high water. I finished it in six months.

"It sold to Doubleday for an advance of $1000! Big money in those days, especially for a first novel. Then the checks began coming in, pre-publication, book clubs, condensations, serial rights, a play offer. I said, What the hell am I working in an office for? I'll write books.

"*The Amboy Dukes* sold substantially, in paperback four or five million copies. On the basis of that book, my Hollywood dream was fulfilled. I was hired by Warner Brothers to do the screenplay. My agent warned me: 'We represent many writers, Hollywood writers. There are more one-book writers in Hollywood than throughout the United States. They write one thing, go there, and they never write again. When the studio tires of them they say, give us a fresh mind. Meanwhile the writer had established himself at a level of expenditure far above his means, and that's tragic.'

"Well, I went out to Hollywood and realized my agent was right. I decided I would continue to write novels. My film work was my avocation. I knew it was ephemeral and you could get wiped out very easily. I saw it happen over and over again to many good writers. Well, I've been here for thirty years. It has struck me as an elaborate game, a masquerade for which I was paid handsomely. I felt overpaid, especially given the contempt which most writers have for writing films. It's crap, and the public wants crap. Give them crap and everyone goes home happy—the moguls, the writers, the public. I worked for Warners, Universal, Republic, Columbia, but I kept writing books. I was pretty lucky in that the writing of books assuaged the emotional pain I felt from writing screenplays only for the money.

"I was recently talking to someone in a publishing company. He told me, 'I'm only interested in signing books that are sure bestsellers.' Good manners intervened—I didn't say to him what I've said in casual conversation. If I had a formula for a best-seller I wouldn't write the book, I'd sell the formula for a million or more! Nobody knows a formula. They're all looking for a big formula. Is it possible to combine *Batman* and *Star Wars*? The formula doesn't exist. Art and money in Hollywood? Everyone will tell you they're really involved with art, when they are all involved with money!"

As a writer, Joseph Wambaugh wasn't able to balance his act as well as Shulman. Money played tricks with his life's calling. Wambaugh was a Marine private, a steelworker, and a Los Angeles cop who wrote in his spare time. He was in over his head financially with car payments, a mortgage, and a food budget until he sold his first novel, *The New Centurions*. He has been on the best-seller list ever since, with a number of later books including *The Onion Field, The Blue Knight,* and in 1989 *The Blooding.* In an interview he commented: "I can't really say that my life has changed that much, except now I have money. I still hang out with cops. My tennis partner is a cop. When I go out socially, when I'm not going out with my wife, I go out with cops and saloon keepers. I do the same things I always did. I do have more time now. When I was a cop, I was always working two jobs and writing. I sold suits out of the back of my car, did shoplifting detail in stores for extra money, and when I got my masters degree, I taught.

"I don't think my life's gotten easier as a result of my success with writing. In fact, it's gotten complicated in a lot of ways. I miss police work a lot. I think probably I was happier as a policeman. Police work got rid of me; I didn't get rid of police work. Everybody treated me so differently because of the wealth and notoriety I received as a writer that finally I was like a freak as a cop. I tried to stick it out, but I couldn't. But I have my fantasies. Every time I drive by a cop who has a suspect I think—that guy is gonna get away and they're gonna need me.

"For the first couple of years I was star-struck. But after personal and financial dealings with publishers and Hollywood people, I became disappointed. If they [the studios] own you, they stop listening to you. I walked away from *Police Story* [the successful TV drama he helped create]. I probably looked arrogant, but I'm not. It's just that I cared about it, not only because of the money it made for me. It's the only way I can deal with people who don't know the material as well as I do, and who don't understand about the cop's way of life and never will."

Like many creative writers, the late novelist, screenwriter, and teacher of writing, Bernard Wolfe never hit it big financially, despite the fact that he published several excellent novels and works of nonfiction like *Trotsky Dead, Really the Blues* and his highly acclaimed Hollywood novel, *Come on out Daddy.* As he talks about his career and money, it becomes clear that he acquired and maintained what he sought after most of all: Artistic integrity over money.

In my interview with him he commented: "I did not become aware of much significance attached to money until the Depression with my father's loss of a job. I began to see the importance of money only after he lost our house and there was no money to feed us. My reaction was outrage! Money seemed to me an imposition. I didn't want to think about money. I resented having to concern myself with money.

"Given my impecunious beginnings, there was a period when I wrote pornography because I desperately needed money to support my parents in a separate establishment. My only reason for writing the stuff, which I despised, was money. It was still the Depression and I couldn't get a job anywhere else. The way it came about was that I became friendly with Henry Miller, who was living in New York at that time. He had connections which, in his usual spirit of incredible generosity, he led me to. In particular, he knew this guy who had this big pornography operation. It was purely a matter of practicality, and, I must say, it was at the time that I became ruthless about money because this guy's standard procedure was to pay fifty cents a page for his pornographic volumes. I came in under Henry Miller's auspices, so I wasn't going to be satisfied with even a dollar a page. I fought and fought and maneuvered and maneuvered, and conned and lied, and got two dollars a page, and ever since then I've known how to maneuver that way. I go after the top dollar whenever I do anything that I'm doing strictly for money. Writing that has personal meaning to me I'll do for nothing.

"I thought the pornography publisher was a swine. I knew he had money. I knew my only reason for having one minute of association with him was to get the maximum amount of money I could from him. The moment I had enough money to get away from him and had other sources of income by getting so-called respectable jobs, I cut him dead and left him with one half of a manuscript, which was unusable. I left him with a cliff-hanger, and I was happy to do it. I've walked away from other situations where money was my only reason for the work—and there was limited literary or artistic value to what I was doing.

"Another unfulfilling writing job I did for money involved working for *Popular Science.* I found I had a real knack for their kind of journalism. I did it with my little finger. I was in no way emotionally involved as a writer of that stuff. Then I saw greener pastures elsewhere. I went to a competitive magazine, *Mechanics Illustrated,* published by an enormous magazine empire, Fawcett Publications. It was clear that I had a talent for this type of work.

"I knew how to deal with people. They were making it very clear to me I had a big career there. The people who stayed and made careers got to be $250,000-a-year executives. I knew that was being offered to me. But I finally got hold of a book project, a very important one, that meant something to me. I was writing it nights and weekends. The moment I got it nailed down with a publisher, I knew I was going to be launched in the publishing world, [so] I went to the Fawcett people and quit. So I turned my back on a very comfortable financial career in a sort of writing that meant very little to me.

"I was thinking when I quit, by incredible luck plus some talent which I'd mobilized to the fullest, I'm liberating myself! I was liberating myself from $250,000 a year, but it seemed like true liberation to me. I tell you today, for all the financial headaches I still have, I continue to look upon it as liberation. I have no regrets for that decision.

"I have no regrets even though these days as a writer I have the severest financial pressures I've had in my life. I'm fighting a battle day to day just to survive. I could go down the financial drain at any moment. Yet I still don't regret having left these shlock writing jobs. I never learned how to develop the skill to make money and write what I want to write—novels.

"A good friend of mine, Saul Bellow, developed his writing skills and has become a multimillionaire. He's a very skillful, very deft, very clever, supremely intelligent guy, there's no question about it, and some of his stylistic writing adventures are a delight. But finally the basic psychological content of his books, I feel, are shoddy. Now, I do know some things about Saul. He started out privileged. His family was very well-off. When his father died, he inherited quite a lot of money. And that made it possible for him to do a lot of things that I can't and don't have the luxury to do as a writer.

"Many writers, like Bellow, are fortunate in that they start out with the great advantage of wealth. Thomas Mann and Andre Gide started out with inherited wealth and could devote themselves full-time to fooling around any way they wanted literarily from their early twenties. Saul Bellow could do that, too. This gives these writers at least an initial advantage—I envy that. I don't envy them individually, but I envy anybody who has serious thrust as a writer, and has the luxury to follow it naturally without the emotional pressure on him to produce money from day to day. In those cases, as writers, their art reigns supreme because they have no money worries.

"Don't misunderstand me. In my current terrible financial straits I would write quite a few shlock things for money. I wouldn't ghost write *Mein Kampf,* but I would do a wide range of things. I'll write any f—ing movie that they ask me to write. In some cases, I might ask them to be awfully nice and leave my name off.

"I'm not oblivious to the large amounts of money made by many of my writer friends and enemies. In fact, I have a sense of wonderment at the great wealth certain people have accumulated through writing—even though I consider some books I've written at least to be of equal value and in some cases better than the money-makers. I know that my most heartfelt, gut-implanted interests and impulses, needs, cravings, are met by what I consider my current writing, which I somehow must do, even with my financial disaster my family and I are now confronting."

What comes across most fervently in Wolfe's interview is the basic need creative people harbor to express themselves. That creative voice can neither be bought nor bought off, no matter how expensive a carrot is dangled in front of them. Artistic integrity and creative fulfillment are more valued than material success. Wolfe, a good friend of mine, accepted with grace and style the financial frustrations and problems that often accompany creative integrity. As he once told me, "If you choose the high road as a writer, it too often goes with the territory."

ARTISTS AND MUSICIANS

In 1989 and 1990, many old masters like Van Gogh and Picasso have been sold and bought for millions of dollars—some for over $100 million. These prices are more money than all of the twentieth century artists combined ever made during their lifetimes. In many cases, artists are notoriously exploited by businesspeople who abound in the art field. The crass money-makers exploit talented artists, rationalizing their behavior with arguments like "artists aren't subject to the same greed." The wheelers and dealers make most of the money, while the artists struggle with the creative process.

Artists play into greedy hands because they ascribe to the old starving-artist mythology, feeling "whorish," impure if they fight for adequate compensation for their works. The prevailing view, which allows for exploitation and greed, says artists are not businesspeople. They should be more concerned with producing quality work than with dollars. Consequently, most artists are usually ineffectual at making money from their valuable creations.

Jane Wayne, both an artist and an art teacher, commented articulately on this state of artistic affairs: "Artists complain about the same old problems year after year no matter how obscure or famous we may be. We ask each other how to get a better gallery, how to move our dealers to promote our works more vigorously. We gossip a lot about museums, too: how a certain trustee collects the art of so-and-so, which explains his retrospective at the Modern; or how a certain young curator is mounting a whole exhibition to prove his pet aesthetic gimmick.

"Sooner or later one of us casually drops the word that Joseph Hirshorn [the influential billionaire who collected billions of dollars' worth of art for his Washington gallery] just blew into town and 'bought out the studio,' but no mention is made of the prices he paid—nor do we ask. We know the idiosyncrasies of all the collectors and we'd just as soon not be reminded of what 'making it' can mean. Artists lick their wounds for nourishment, not for healing.

"Over the years, I have pondered why guilds and royalties never developed for visual artists. Perhaps because we are unworldly about the practical matters of sales and careers. Neither art schools nor university art departments provide courses in the business and professional problems of being an artist. A master's degree may qualify the student to replace the teacher but not to bargain with a dealer.

"A union or guild needs an industry against which to organize, but the art scene has no single nexus of power to bargain with. As for the public agencies, they dissolve into lay committees which have neither the concern nor the authority to address the grievances of artists. The art world lives in an ebb and flow of guerilla warfare. Such citadels of power as there are—museums, foundations, art councils, the National Endowments—are held by *them*, not *us*, and only rarely can one find an artist who is a member of one of their committees. So we learn very early to see ourselves as aesthetically unique and morally superior, which is a palatable way of saying isolated and powerless. And, I would add, usually broke and exploited.

"In the relationship between money and art, money enjoys short-term advantage. Money compels attention, and therefore changes what we see and the way we see it. Yet, in the end, art somehow survives the money."

Even in Ms. Wayne's astute remarks you can detect the artistic talent for rationalization as she focuses on the long view of art objects, and the fickle public judgments and price tags. Every one knows most artists are not properly appreciated or compensated in their own lifetimes. True artists are supposed to be dedicated to their art, not to their pocketbooks, and so the issue of money continues to be evaded and eluded and left to those less artistically talented and more coldly entrepreneurially oriented.

Although musicians live in a world where royalties are tabulated by ASCAP and where the industry is the record industry, less fragmented than the art world of dealers, foundations, and collectors, they, too, have historically been left out of commercial affairs and oftentimes fair profits.

In recent years we've heard biography after biography of singers and songwriters like Little Richard, Mary Wilson of the Supremes, Brian Wilson of the Beach Boys, and even the Beatles who report making little or unfair incomes based on their music's popularity and overall earning power. It's common knowledge that musicians from Elvis on down were commercially exploited by profiteers ranging from managers to record companies.

The Beatles are periodically engaged in a lawsuit against record companies over royalties. Some of their comments reflect how musicians, even famous successful ones, avoid the subject of money, earnings, and accountability.

Ringo Starr: "I never talked business with Brian [Brian Epstein, their longtime manager]. Brian was the manager. We are not businessmen. We are musicians. That was our game."

George Harrison: "You have to realize at the time I had given my trust to this man [Allen Klein, a manager who succeeded Epstein and was removed two years later for defrauding the group]. I was hoping that he was looking out for me. I did not want to be involved in the hassle of business because I was trying to be an artist."

After Epstein's death, the Beatles did try to form and run their own production company, which they called Apple. Their financial fiasco is now legendary, and was instrumental in their break-up and in the court case which has been ongoing for a decade. Like many musicians, the Beatles didn't want to be businessmen, but realized (too late) that business acumen can be just as crucial as talent to their personal success and for the avoidance of the emotional agony of suing for one's just renumeration.

This lesson, learned at the expense of generations of musicians, from Beethoven to the Beatles, is clear to most contemporary musicians. Today's musicians realize the music business is more than just music. It is reading the fine print in contracts, fighting for accounting details and distribution figures. Now musicians arm themselves with lawyers and accountants as well as agents. In the 1960s, musicians and rock stars were renegades, "above commerce" if not riding in limos. Today's breed is money-conscious, competing among themselves to be spokespersons for commerce, anxious to promote an array of products from soft drinks to sneakers to stereo systems. Some believe this to be crass, others smart—and so goes the emotional battle over money and art. The ultimate question: Whose business is it making money anyway, the agent's or the artist's?

THEATER AND FILM

Paradoxically, some creative artists in film trade on their talent and have little to show—no artistic pay-off. meantime, the businesspeople profit. As the old Hollywood saying goes: "Many deals, few pictures."

A well-known screen and TV writer who wanted to be anonymous had this peculiar dilemma of being used financially, making considerable money himself and yet having no artistic product.

"You know, Lew, the last picture of mine that was filmed was ten years ago. Since that time I've made several million dollars. My wife, four kids, and I have lived in style for these years—yet I've dried up inside because nothing good that I've written has been up there on the screen with my name on it. I get no emotional satisfaction from the practice of making deals and money. My gratification is acquired from seeing my best film product get out into the world.

"So here I sit grinding things out—not always what I want to write—and two of my kids have never in their lifetime seen my name up there on anything. It kills me. They know I'm a writer, because they see me at my desk writing every day. And they know that my work is acknowledged by important people in this town—yet in their lifetime they have not seen my name up on that screen on a production. I'm making money, but that's certainly not my main goal in life, nor do I get any emotional gratification from this sterile money game."

In brief, despite his sizable income, this writer had no product results. On one occasion he facetiously told me: "I recently received $100,000 for a first draft screenplay on a film that will probably never be made. I wrote a letter to the producer in which I told him the next time I write a screenplay for you that isn't made, it's going to cost you $200,000."

No one case of an artist and his money reveals the complex and intriguing relationship than the head-on battle that resulted from Ingmar Bergman's conflict with his country. Bergman's case reveals much of the emotional meaning of money in the life of an artist, and the manner in which the creative artist's process and identity can be crushed by economic issues. In a highly publicized tax case, Bergman was ignominiously arrested while rehearsing a play, *The Dance of Death,* at the Royal Dramatic Theater, and charged with tax fraud to the tune of

$750,000. In an open letter explaining why he was leaving his native Sweden because of this financial problem, Bergman, the ultimate film artist, wrote:

"I realized that anyone in this country, any time and in any way, can be attacked and vilified by a particular kind of bureaucracy that grows like a galloping cancer. Money and things are indifferent to me; always have been and always will be—now more than ever. I feel no anxiety about losing everything I own in a court case. I don't measure my assets in money or things. I felt that I had been ill-treated and shamed, but I felt that I had to ignore this to be able to return to reality and my work. . . . For the first time in my adult life, a paralysis has seized me and carried me further into a depression that looks more and more like an identity crisis. If I don't create, I don't exist. The paralyzing feeling of insecurity I have lived with in the last few months must be brought to an end. If I cannot work, my life is meaningless."

Bergman's reality was the creative process, not profit. His huge artistic pay-offs, his profits, got him into financial trouble, although the charges were later dropped. Ironically, his success sabotaged his creativity because he did not properly concern himself with money, and only with his art.

Apparently money is irrelevant to an artist like Bergman. However, his ignorance of its dynamics produced a dreadful situation for him and his artistry. His case is pehaps more dramatic than most, yet has a prototypical quality that holds true for those artists who see their work as their life.

Actors and actresses have money problems, too, which can plague them all their lives. They have their own version of the trash versus art controversy, pitting box office appeal against serious acting ability, blockbuster films and sequels against "good" films. There is a hierarchy set up throughout the acting community with dubbing TV or doing commercials being bottom of the barrel jobs. Films and stage work are the most prestigious jobs, artistically speaking.

Money is a multifaceted emotional dilemma for many. Too much money as well as too little can be problematic. Actors and actresses inundated with fame and fortune complain about their loss of privacy and normalcy, and the enormous pressure of success.

Most actors and actresses fall into this poverty-stricken category.

About 3 percent of the approximate 40,000 members of the Screen Actors Guild ever earn over $50,000 annually. About 1 percent of SAG members earn over $100,000 from their acting. The rest are struggling at jobs to supplement their incomes, hoping an acting opportunity will appear on the horizon. Remember, a person who is a member of SAG has already "made it," there are tens of thousands of actors in the United States who never even get into the union.

Several years ago I was invited by SAG to deliver a lecture which they entitled "The Occupational Hazards of Acting as a Career." Two major points I made involved: (1) the built-in rejection of the actor's role, and (2) the poverty with which most actors/actresses must contend. I taped the session, and it provided me with some interesting feedback on money issues and actors.

Actors and actresses tend to emotionally rationalize the poverty factor in their profession. They rationalize, finding some good coming out of their poverty: One forty-year-old actress commented, after I had talked at SAG about the rejection and poverty that is entwined with the acting profession, as follows: "In order to pursue my acting career, I had to find other work as a waitress or secretary to bring in steady income. As an actress I have to *know* what happens to other people, how they live, and believe me, I've known poverty because I've lived it as an actress!" For this woman, poverty was a good training ground. Since the Actor's Studio or some such workshop experience wasn't available, she reframed her life in a constructive way to help her talent.

Another popular rationale that came out of my lecture and discussion with the group involved their raising the enormous amount of *rejection* they endured in casting for a role at an audition to the level of a virtue. A young actress was upset by my comment that a persistent occupational emotional hazard of being an actor was a considerable amount of built-in rejection. I said: "After all, most actors and actresses audition for hundreds of parts before they get one. They are rejected at least ninety-nine times out of a hundred."

The actress responded: "I think the point you made about a 'baptism of fire' is something I've experienced, and I think a lot of the problems actors have shouldn't be problems—we view them as problems. They aren't problems, they are strengths. The confidence to face rejection and feel rejection is something not to be proud of necessarily, but something to be committed to. We tend to experience rejection as a negative instead of saying to ourselves: 'I was rejected, but I had the courage to go out and try to get that job.' We should look at ourselves as very courageous people who know how to live with rejection and poverty."

The sustained applause that followed this actress's testimony appeared to be directed at me for even bringing up rejection—what I viewed as a rationalization of the debatable merits of rejection—and attested to the fact that the audience related to her experience. I meanly responded: "You may feel rejection and poverty is courageous and toughens you up, but I feel you would be better off getting every part you're up for."

Elevating things like rejection or poverty to virtues like valor smacks of a kind of martyrdom and rationalization. Many actors and actresses fight to survive just for an occasional chance to exhibit their talent. They will suffer much just to engage in the dramatic process. Profit isn't even a consideration, but for many just a fantasy. Why suffer so? As one drama addict put it, "If I wanted a dull life I wouldn't want to be an actress!"

ATHLETES—CASHING IN ON TALENT

Although athletes may not be creative artists in the strictest sense, their natural talents enhanced by years of training in the ring, the ball field or on the basketball court are definitely those of performance artists. Sports and sports stars have become a big part of the entertainment business. People will pay high prices to see certain sports figures demonstrate their talents.

Perhaps no other segment of the performing arts community has been so effective at parlaying talent into millions than sports stars. Is Mike Tyson worth $20 million for a single fight, an amount he has earned for a championship duel? Orel Hershhiser, Kareem, Magic, Dwight Gooden, Roger Staubach and countless other football, basketball, baseball, hockey, tennis champions and on, generate a packed audience—and so sports promoters and team owners are willing to pay handsomely. Talented athletes earn reasonable to unreasonable amounts of money for their skills.

How have athletes managed to cash in on their talents so profitably? Professional athletes often point out the shortness of their careers and the toll it takes on them physically as a basis for getting a maximum amount of revenue during their box office heyday. Many players in contact sports leave the game physically damaged, especially football players, who often retire from pro football partially crippled. Some sports heroes and heroines can translate their fame into other careers such as broadcasting, restaurants, or advertising. Yet there will always be the classic cases like the punch-drunk prizefighter who will go another couple of rounds for the money, long after his career (and his stamina) has peaked. The greatest fighter of all times, Joe Louis, departed the ring as a comic wrestler, and in his later years became a Las Vegas "greeter" for the money he needed to live on.

While it is usual to talk about sports and sports figures with reverence, it's naive to underestimate the impact of money on the game. Some sports celebrities may be reluctant to admit they are "in it for the money," but not all. A defensive tackle for an NFL team, who wanted anonymity, was candid and honest in an interview on playing the game and money.

When asked what keeps him playing, he responded, "Money. Some people still feel the mystique and excitement of it, but money's why we are all playing, right? Maybe there is something wrong with me. After ten years, the magic is gone.

"It's a job and a good job. I get enjoyment out of overcoming my fears, my inabilities and my perceived inabilities. That's interesting and challenging. That's what makes me able to do what I do. But basically, it's the money. If it wasn't for the money, I sure could do a lot of other things.

"People who pay money to watch football games, for whatever reasons, are entitled to the best performance I can give them. That's the only area where I've got control.

"There is showmanship involved. I think of myself as an entertainer-artist, more artist than entertainer. We have some talents that are different from other people's. Other people have some talents that we don't have."

Money is a major determinant, if not *the* major one, in what athletes do. Team spirit and team loyalty appears to be passé in today's sports world. When Carl Finley, owner of the Oakland A's baseball team, initially attempted to sell several of his star players for around a million a piece, there was an outcry from fans and players about the crassness of such an act! Now in the era of free agents, most athletes bargain for the most money they can get, with loyalty to a team being old hat. I am always amazed at how a lifetime L.A. Dodger like Steve Garvey can alter play for their arch rival, the San Diego Padres, without much change in performance or loyalty. Money is the factor.

TELEVISION NEWS—MASS MEDIA MILLIONAIRES

The charisma and presence of certain individuals on television produces excellent ratings, which mean high advertising revenues. Why else would an Oprah Winfrey, a Barbara Walters, or a Geraldo Rivera be paid such large sums? Money talk makes many a newsroom hum, behind the scenes if not on camera.

Are million-dollar anchorpeople and TV stars like Brokaw, Walters, or Rather worth their weight in gold? More conservative financial management in the TV business is now pulling in the reins on star journalists. This and other controversies are rooted in money. The most talked-about battle of the media news stars is the conflict between expertise and good luck, as portrayed in the popular movie *Broadcast News,* a variation on the trash versus art theme, only in a more personal context—pretty boy/pretty girl flash versus substantive serious reporting is the new theme. The cold hard cash reality is that charismatic personalities with stage presence rise to the top of the journalistic heap with or without legitimate credentials.

Should reporting the news be a public service or an entertainment spot, a question explored by Paddy Chayefsky in the classic film *Network.* Old school journalists see it one way. Frank is one of these. He sees his career as service-oriented and ranks money unimportant in contrast to the significance of his work.

"Money doesn't mean a hell of a lot to me. What the hell, the check has to go so many ways that I don't even worry about it anymore. I wouldn't give up this life for anything, because news-producing is the most satisfying work I've ever done. What good is making a lot of money when you're not happy doing what you're doing? I know some guys on the lot who are making a fortune every year and are as unhappy as hell.

"There are many other things that are more important than money. The first is health. Love and respect are also a hell of a lot more important than money. Without love, where are you? Nowhere. I know that song well. The same thing with respect—both for yourself and the respect of others for you. Without that, you're not worth a damn thing. I think I'm well respected, and that means more to me than all the money in this town.

"My parents placed a lot of importance on money. I was raised in a Catholic section of a midwestern city, attended church schools until I reached college. At that time I worked as a copyboy for a large midwestern daily paper, then became a sportswriter. Eventually I went over to television. Several years later I migrated to sunny Southern California. You never know what fame and the pursuit of the buck will do to people.

"Some people I've seen in this business are totally unchanged by fame. Others get eaten alive by it. I don't think that would happen to me, but there is absolutely no way of predicting what will happen. So the biggest part of my life is spent doing what I believe is creative work at the studio."

The old school of hard-driving legitimate reporters is declining in many instances because ratings make more profits than idealism. The challenge for the TV journalists of the 90s is to combine good reporting and important stories with material mass appeal. Navigating such a course is not easy. But some, like Geraldo Rivera, have been able in their careers to cut the "ideal" deal, and do exactly what they like to do for big money.

Rivera, a lawyer-activist, broke into TV journalism when networks were looking to balance out their ethnic mix of staff. Of his early ABC Eyewitness News hiring in New York, he said:

"They hired me early on not because I was bright or an attorney but a Puerto Rican who's not too offensive looking and not too short." (In fact, Geraldo's mother is Jewish and his father is Puerto Rican.)

Rivera has successfully combined on-camera braggadocio and confrontation tactics with idealism whether he is reporting from war zones or urban ghettoes. His career had its ups and downs, but his popularity is enormous. His job hosting a daily syndicated talk show, regular specials of documentary nature, and entertainment news reports for Fox makes him one of the highest paid TV journalists in the business.

Of his talent for balancing the idealistic with the materialistic appeal of the news business, he commented in a recent interview: "I'm a self-defined pragmatic idealist. I think if I were only an idealist I would never have survived. The point is, there are things you have to do, and you do the best you can in the balance between morality and the need to be commercially appealing." Rivera, like many people engaged in the creative arts, has created a compromise between the realities of the marketplace and his creative identity.

Money and the concern with it doesn't have to be the kiss of death in the creative arts. For example, millionaire J. Paul Getty contributed enormously to the art world by creating the Getty Museum. While most tycoons left their fortunes to conventional charities, Getty's life intention was to provide California and the world with a museum—an architectural art in its own right—in which his astounding art collection would be displayed. The J. Paul Getty Museum, nestled in the sloping hills of his Malibu estate, features Renaissance and Baroque paintings, and 18th Century French decorative arts which so fascinated Getty, and many of which he "picked up" from the Rothchilds. The big draw is the building and the setting, pure Mediterranean, an almost exact copy of an ancient Roman seaside villa encased on molten lava-mud when Mt. Vesuvius erupted in 79 A.D. and destroyed the town of Herculaneum. Getty's will ensured millions in endowments to be converted to art substance and enjoyed in perpetuity.

Many creative projects, as was pointed out earlier related to Shakespeare's "Hamlet," in part conceived just for the money have been classified as classics. Another example of how art emerged from monetary needs is William Faulkner's novel *Sanctuary*. Faulkner was forced by financial straits to move from his beloved Mississippi to Hollywood strictly to earn some money. His first four books including *The Sound and the Fury* sold poorly. For a time in his late twenties he earned his money doing handyman jobs. This all changed after his marriage in 1929 when he changed his philosophy.

Faulkner said, "I began to think of books in terms of possible money. I decided I might just as well make some of it myself. I took a little time out and speculated what a person in Mississippi would believe to be current trends and invented the most horrific tale I could imagine. I wrote the book in about three weeks and sent it to Smith [his publisher], who wrote me immediately, 'Good God, I can't publish this. We'd both be in jail."

Later, Smith changed his mind and printed galleys and sent them off to Faulkner. In a letter to a friend, Faulkner revealed his feelings about his concocted *Sanctuary:* "I saw that it was so terrible that there were two things to do, tear it up or rewrite it. I thought again, 'It might sell! Maybe ten thousand people will buy it.' So I tore the galleys down and rewrote the book, trying to make out of it something which would not shame *The Sound and the Fury* and *As I Lay Dying* too much. I made a fair job, and I hope you will buy it and tell your friends to buy it too."

As it turned out for Faulkner, "fair job" was an understatement. His Sanctuary, conceived primarily for profit, became a classic that has sold millions of copies. The same fate was destined for what was perceived back then by Fitzgerald as magazine "trash," written by him for money. This "trash" is now in classic literary anthologies which have sold millions of copies. The distinction creative people make in their minds between trash and art is often not made by the public. Commercial ventures like *Gone with the Wind* rise above initial market strategies. Pop art collections like Andy Warhol's out-price themselves over and over again in the public's desire to see them. Since his death Warhol's pop art has sold for millions.

Money is not a simple matter for creative people. Art versus trash, or selling-out is too often seen in terms of black and white. In truth, the relationship among the creative arts, talent, and money is a significant and complex issue. Money can corrupt creative people or help them to be more creative—if they keep the money factor in its proper perspective. This issue of money in its proper perspective is a truism that everyone should incorporate into their lives. If money and the emotions that surround its getting and spending were kept in a logical balance, most of the social problems that exist in our society would be resolved.

Research Notes on Attitudes About Money

*T*HIS FINAL section of the book is presented for those readers interested in my research approach, and a more detailed analysis and interpretation of some of my statistical research findings.

THE RESEARCH APPROACH

The first phase of my research into money involved in-depth interviews with over fifty people from all walks of life. All of the interviews lasted at least an hour and probed issues such as the respondents' early life experiences with money, parental influence on attitudes toward money, viewpoints on credit, marital money situations, and most depressing and happiest experiences with money, and their basic mode of adaptation or money style. These varied interviews were carried out alongside a comprehensive review of the research and literature on the subject.

In my survey of the literature on money, I found very little hard information on people's attitudes about the emotional meaning of money in their lives. Given the limited state of hard knowledge on the subject, I felt it was necessary systematically to obtain current data on the specific subject of people's emotional attitudes about money, beyond the in-depth interviews I had done.

The second phase of my research involved a comprehensive survey of 410 people from all walks of life. The survey was randomly administered by a team of more than a hundred sociology students and professional colleagues of mine in several geographic locations including the East Coast, the Midwest, and dominantly in Southern California, and resulted in a geographically national sample of people. An effort was made to acquire a reasonable proportion of responses from various ethnic, religious, occupational, income, and educational categories of people. The sample consisted of 210 men and 200 women (men 52 percent, women 48 percent). The average age in the total sample was thirty-two. There were 219 married people (53 percent) and 178 single people (43 percent). In terms of occupation, there were 202 white collar workers, 70 blue collar workers, and 172 students and housewives.

The questions developed for the survey were based on issues that repeatedly emerged in the more free-swinging in-depth interviews. They encompass the emotional meaning of money in several broad areas: the effect of money on people's emotional *condition;* the role of credit in people's lives; how money affects people's romance, sex life, and marriage; how people are socialized into their attitudes on money by their parents; the importance of money in a person's occupation; and people's different modes of adaptation to money. The specific questionnaire used is presented here in its entirety, even though for various reasons not all of the questions yielded responses that are analyzed here in the Appendix.

QUESTIONNAIRE

With the aid of several assistants, I am carrying out a survey into people's emotions about money and how these feelings affect their lives. I appreciate your help in supplying information about this important aspect of human behavior.

Dr. Lewis Yablonsky, PROFESSOR OF SOCIOLOGY
CALIFORNIA STATE UNIVERSITY, NORTHRIDGE, CALIFORNIA

1. Age _____

2. ☐ Male
   ☐ Female

3. ☐ Married
   ☐ Single
   ☐ Living with spouse

4. Occupation _____

5. Education completed _____

6. Religion _____

7. *Annual* income/family _____

8. Describe your first significant memory of money, as a child.

9. How does money affect your emotional condition? (positive and negative emotions)

10. Relate the *most depressing* and the *happiest* experience you have ever had with money.

11. Do you feel you are reasonably "sensible" in your handling of money? Check one:
    ☐ Very sensible
    ☐ Sensible
    ☐ Foolish
    Explain:

12. How do you feel about "credit" in your life? Check one:
    ☐ It is useful to me
    ☐ I let it get out of hand
    Explain:

13. What is your *emotional experience* related to gambling with money? (either in a game of chance, on real estate, or in the stock market)

14. Has money in any way affected your romantic relationships? How?

15. Have you or would you marry (or live with) someone mainly because of their financial position?
    ☐ Yes
    ☐ No
    Explain:

16. If you are married (or divorced), do you (or did you) and your spouse share the same views on money?
    ☐ Yes
    ☐ No
    Explain:

17. Do you (or if divorced, did you) argue or fight with your spouse over money matters? Check one:
    ☐ Never
    ☐ Seldom
    ☐ Often
    ☐ Constantly
    Briefly explain:

18. Has money affected your sex life?
    ☐ Yes
    ☐ No
    How?

19. In your opinion, what is the best way to teach children the value of money?

20. How were you taught about money by your parents?

21. Has your relationship with your parents, or your relationships with your children, been affected by money? How?

22. How much emphasis did your parents place on your being financially successful? Check one:
    ☐ Great emphasis
    ☐ Little emphasis
    ☐ No emphasis

    Have you fulfilled their expectations?
    ☐ Yes
    ☐ No
    Explain:

23. How important is money to you in your occupational aspirations? Check one:
    ☐ Money is the only reason for me to work
    ☐ Money is important but my work is important too
    ☐ I like my work and money is of secondary importance
    ☐ Other
    Explain:

24. *Modes of Adaptation to Money:* Following are several emotional postures related to money. Read all of them and check the ones that most closely fits your lifestyle and point of view on money.

    A. ☐ I am generally content with whatever my money, power, and success position happens to be.

    B. ☐ I have logical and achievable financial-power-success goals and can (or have) acquired the financial status I seek.

    C. ☐ I strive to attain all the money, power, and success I can, yet I do not let my money struggle, my success or lack of success negatively affect my emotional condition.

    D. ☐ I strive for an ideal, and possibly achievable high level of financial power and success, and suffer great emotional pain because I have not yet achieved my desired goal of financial power and success.

    E. ☐ The level of money, power, success I seek always seems to be the next higher level of the ladder. There always seems to be a gap between what I want and what I have. I am usually in a state of emotional pain, and have a sense of deprivation no matter how much I seem to get.

    F. ☐ Other (if none of the foregoing apply to you, describe your own situation).

    G. ☐ Explain why you selected the category you checked.

25. You inherit five million dollars (after taxes). What would you do with it? How would it emotionally affect your life and change your lifestyle?

A SUMMARY ANALYSIS OF RESPONSES

Following are the findings on specific questions that lent themselves to quantitative percentage answers and analysis. Only the questions and responses which appeared to have some validity are analyzed here. The qualitative questions (such as, "Relate the most *depressing* and *happiest* experience you ever had with money") were analyzed in relevant places throughout the book. In the following data analysis, where the total is not 410 it is explained by the fact that some people did not respond to all of the questions.

- **Question 11: Do you feel you are reasonably sensible in handling money?**

People rated themselves as follows:

Category Label	Number	Percent
Very sensible	124	30.2
Sensible	246	60.0
Foolish	38	9.3
Not Responsible	2	.5
TOTALS	410	100

Age and Handling Money

In correlating our data with other factors, I found that a significant relationship existed between age and money. Younger people felt they were much less sensible in handling money than older people. Interestingly, *no one* over fifty believed that he or she handled money foolishly.

Education and Handling Money

There was a definite correlation between people's self-perceived sensibility in handling money and their educational level. People with less education, particularly those who hadn't finished high school, were much more likely to consider their spending of money as foolish than those who had completed high school. And college graduates felt they were more sensible than high school level people.

This is a finding that has many implications. People who have more education generally earn more money and are more judicious in handling their money. Whereas less educated, poorer people, are more apt to be foolish in handling the little money that they have. The platitude "the rich get richer and the poor get poorer" is in part validated by this finding in my research.

Gender and Handling Money

We found a clear pattern of difference between the male and female self-concept on their handling of money. More men than statistically expected and fewer women than statistically expected felt they handled money sensibly. From the responses, we can conclude that women in general feel they do not handle money as sensibly as men.

The younger the women, the more prevalent the feeling that they handle money foolishly. Teenage girls consider themselves the most foolish in handling money. This may in part be due to peer fad and fashion pressures.

The cultural processes may play a significant role in women's feeling they aren't sensible in handling money. There appears to be a higher general expectation that young boys should learn "the value of a dollar." And parents may be more indulgent in spending money on their teenage daughters than on their teenage sons.

- ### Question 12: How do you feel about credit in your life?

This question was posed because increasingly people complain about credit and the manner in which it gets out of hand in their lives. Surprisingly, about 70 percent of those surveyed felt that credit was useful in their lives; and only 21 percent (87) felt it was not useful.

With regard to the more fundamental issue of whether people let credit get out of hand, 90 percent felt they were in control of the credit situation in their lives, and only 10 percent felt it was out of hand. This perception does not jibe with the perceptions of people who are in the business of money management.

We can conclude from the data that credit is a valuable and useful adjunct to the financial lives of people in contemporary society. And despite the fact that many people have misgivings about credit, they are able to effectively incorporate it into their lifestyle, even though they appear to misjudge the degree to which it is "out of hand" in their lives.

- ### *Question 15: Have you or would you marry (or live with) someone for money?*

There are innumerable success stories in American folklore and literature on the virtues of lifting oneself into a higher status by a "good" (that is, financially "good") marriage. Yet 81 percent of the sample reject this means of upper mobility. Apparently the admonition of many parents that "You can just as easily fall in love with a rich girl-boy as a poor girl-boy" tends to be rejected by most people.

- ### *Question 16: If you are married (or divorced) do you (or did you) and your spouse share the same views on money?*

Interestingly, around 148 people, or 36 percent of the sample, "did not know" the answer to this question. Of those who responded definitely (yes or no) to this question, 162 responded yes and 100 responded no. In the group who responded clearly, therefore, 62 percent of married couples believed they shared similar views on money and 38 percent did not.

A direct and significant statistical relationship exists between gender and the belief that their spouse shares the same views they have about money. Significantly, more married men than married women say they have a different view on money than their spouses. Significantly more females than men responded that they shared the same view on money as their spouses.

Men and women vary with respect to whether or not their spouses share same views on money matters—women seem to believe their views on money are concordant with those of their husbands—while husbands tend to believe the views are dissonant with those of their wives.

Perhaps women rationalize their spending the family's money by contending that their husbands approve—when in fact their husbands don't, but simply keep quiet about their true feelings. In brief, married men seem to disagree with their wives' viewpoint on money; however, many wives "act as if" they share similar views with their husbands.

- **Question 17: Do you (or if divorced, did you) argue or fight with your spouse over money?**

Out of the 410 people surveyed, 135 people did not respond to this question. The breakdown for those who did respond was as follows:

Response	Number	Percent
Never	77	28
Seldom	146	53
Often	41	16
Constantly	11	3
TOTALS	275	100

Only 28 percent claim they never fight with their spouse over money. As might be expected, a cross-tabulation analysis of the data revealed that a significantly higher percentage of married couples who are dissonant or disagree with each other's viewpoint about money, *fight* over money. And the reverse factor is true: The married people who share a *similar* viewpoint about money hardly ever fight about or have conflict over money.

Although my data is incomplete on this, I would speculate that a couple's viewpoint about money is a highly significant element in their marriage, that the ensuing fighting of people operating from different viewpoints produces a higher divorce rate, and that people contemplating marriage should determine beforehand if they share similar money values.

Age and Fighting Over Money

There is a significant relationship between age and the degree to which an individual fights over money with his/her spouse. In the forties age bracket significantly fewer people than expected said they "never fight" with their spouse over money matters and significantly more than expected said they constantly fight with their spouse over money. Married people in their forties are, therefore, more apt to fight over money. I would speculate that these couples use money as a battleground for other problems in their lives at this stage of their married lives.

In general, people in their forties are going through a difficult "passage" in life. It may not be so much the fact that they *disagree* on *money* as they use the money factor as a battleground for resolving other emotional problems in their individual lives. Divorce rates are higher during the forties—people are going through a change of life—marriages become stale. People are looking for reasons to fight and money can provide an opportune battlefield.

Significantly, more people than expected in their fifties and over indicated that they never fight with their spouse over money.

Educational Level and Fighting Over Money

Cross-tabulation of the data reveals an inverse relationship between the frequency of arguments over money between spouses and the education of those spouses. In other words, the higher the educational level, the less likely there are to be fights between spouses over money. Specifically, my research found that: people with less than a high school education are more apt to argue often over money than expected; those with a high school education are more likely to argue constantly over money; and those with a college degree are much less likely to argue over money.

The general interpretation of this matrix is somewhat rhetorical. Those who have better educations are more likely to have better jobs and, consequently, more money, and perhaps less reason to fight over money. Also, we can speculate that "education" per se may make some people wiser and more effective in the handling of money and consequently less inclined to fight.

Further, people with more education may be better integrated into the society and generally have fewer negative emotional issues impinging on their lives; whereas, less educated people are more apt to be poor and struggling with their daily existence. Money can, therefore, become the battleground for fighting over the many other issues which are bothering them.

- **Question 22: How much emphasis did your parents place on your being financially successful? Have you fulfilled their expectations?**

The responses to the first part of the question broke down as follows:

Response	Number	Percent
Great emphasis	123	30
Little emphasis	196	48
No emphasis	66	16
No response	25	6
TOTALS	410	100

It is significant that almost 80 percent of my sample felt that when they were children their parents placed some emphasis on their earning money. This is, of course, to be expected in a money- and success-oriented society.

With regard to the second part of this question, "Have you fulfilled their expectations," I found the following breakdown for those who responded:

Response	Number	Percent
Yes	213	75
No	68	25
TOTALS	271	100

The fact that 75 percent of the respondents felt they had fulfilled their parents' expectations may simply reveal that their individual level of aspiration is congruent with their parents' expectations. Parental influence over their children is clearly as strong in the financial area as research has shown it to be in other areas of life. People operate in terms of their reference group financially, and most people's reference group is their family.

- ***Question 23: How important is money in your occupational aspirations?***

The breakdown was as follows for the 375 who responded:

Response	Number	Percent
Money is the only reason for me to work.	27	8
Money is important, but my work is important too.	116	30
I like my work, and money is of secondary importance.	232	62
TOTALS	375	100

It is surprising to find that over 90 percent of the respondents did not feel that money was their only reason for working. This factor may be a primary indicator of a reasonably healthy society with regard to money and occupation. However, more people in the lower education brackets checked the category "money is the only reason for me to work" than people in the higher education brackets. This may be because menial, assembly-line jobs are less emotionally satisfying than more creative, diverse, or interesting occupations.

References

CHAPTER 1

[1] Lewis Yablonsky, *The Hippie Trip* (Penguin, 1968).
[2] Associated Press, *The Los Angeles Times,* June 4, 1975.
[3] James Knight, *For the Love of Money* (Viking, 1976).

CHAPTER 2

[1] "For the Love of Money," *People,* May 2, 1988.
[2] Harvey Cleckley, *The Mask of Sanity* (Moseby Press, 19).

CHAPTER 3

[1] Jane Lazone, "The High Cost of Living Off Someone Else," *Ms. Magazine,* January 15, 1981.
[2] Paul Frish and Ann Frish, "Sexual Performance and Money," *The New York Times,* November 23, 1986.
[3] Vivian Gornick, "The Price of Paying Your Own Way," *The Village Voice,* September 15, 1983.

[4] Annette Liberman and Vicki Lindner, *Unbalanced Accounts: Why Women Are Still Afraid of Money* (The Atlantic Monthly Press, 1987).

CHAPTER 4

[1] Pepper Schwartz and Philip Blumstein, *American Couples* (William Morrow, 1983).

[2] David H. Olsen's research is reported by Martha Weinman Lear in "The New Marital Therapy," *The New York Times,* March 6, 1988.

[3] Schwartz and Blumstein, *American Couples.*

[4] Ibid.

CHAPTER 5

[1] Lawrence Kutner, "Parent and Child," *The New York Times,* March 18, 1988.

[2] Dr. Roy Grinker, Jr.'s research is reported in "Children of the Wealthy," *The New York Times,* November 23, 1983.

[3] Jerald Bachman, Lloyd Johnson, and Patrick O'Malley, "An Eye on the Future," *Psychology Today,* July, 1987.

[4] A. Astin, "The One Who Has the Most Toys When He Dies Wins," *Psychology Today,* May, 1987.

[5] Ibid.

CHAPTER 6

[1] James Wixen, *Children of the Rich* (Lyle Stuart, 1979).

[2] Roy Grinker, Jr., reported in "Children of the Wealthy."

[3] Associated Press, "Lifestyles of the Rich and Miserable," *Los Angeles Herald Examiner,* January 12, 1987.

[4] This and the following account of Donald Trump is derived from *Time* magazine, January 16, 1989.

CHAPTER 7

[1] Louis Harris, *Inside America* (Vintage, 1987).

CHAPTER 8

[1] William A. Bonger, *Criminality and Economic Conditions* (Little Brown, 1916).

[2] Albert K. Cohen, *Delinquent Boys* (The Free Press, 1955).

[3] David Matza, *Delinquency and Drift* (Wiley, 1966).

[4] "Why Pick on Pete," *Time* magazine, July 10, 1989.

[5] Peter Kerr, "Crack at Retail: Experiences of Three Former Dealers," The *New York Times,* August 2, 1988.

ABOUT THE AUTHOR

Lewis Yablonsky, Ph.D., is a noted professor of sociology at California State University whose widely praised works include fifteen books on such topics as crime and delinquency, family, substance abuse, psychodrama, and the 1960's counterculture. They have been written about in *Time, People,* and other national magazines. Dr. Yablonsky received the "Outstanding Professor Award" selected from 10,000 professors from the California State University system. He has appeared on national shows such as Donahue, Geraldo Rivera, and Oprah Winfrey.